Ireland's Bridges

Bridges ought to have the self-same qualifications as we judge necessary to all other buildings, that they should be commodious, beautiful and lasting.
(Palladio)

The Authors

Dr Ronald Cox is an engineering historian and Director of the Centre for Civil Engineering Heritage at Trinity College Dublin, which he founded in 1995. He has published widely in the fields of civil engineering heritage and engineering biography. He is currently Chairperson of the Heritage Society of the Institution of Engineers of Ireland and of the Industrial Heritage Association of Ireland. He is a member of the Panel for Historic Engineering Works (PHEW) of the Institution of Civil Engineers.

Dr Michael Gould is an engineering historian based in Belfast and has published widely in the fields of general and historical civil engineering and local government administration. He is a former member of the Historic Buildings Council for Northern Ireland and is also a member of PHEW.

Both authors come from an academic background and have together published joint papers on a number of aspects of civil engineering history and heritage. Their seminal work *Civil Engineering Heritage: Ireland* was published by Thomas Telford Publications, London in 1998. ❖

IRELAND'S BRIDGES

RONALD COX • MICHAEL GOULD

WOLFHOUND PRESS

First published in 2003 by
Wolfhound Press
An Imprint of Merlin Publishing
16 Upper Pembroke Street
Dublin 2, Ireland
Tel: +353 1 676 4373
Fax: +353 1 676 4368
publishing@merlin.ie
www.merlin-publishing.com

ISBN 0-86327-864-7

A CIP catalogue record for this book is available
from the British Library.

5 4 3 2 1

Cover and Interior Design by Faye Keegan Design
Printed and bound in Edelvives, Spain.

CONTENTS

Conversion Charts

Imperial units have been used in relation to all bridges erected prior to 1970, at which time the Irish construction industry adopted the metric system of units. Metric units have been used in relation to bridges erected after that date. ❖

The following approximate conversion factors may be used:

1 yard = 0.9m
1 inch = 25mm
1 mile = 1.6km
1 foot = 0.3m

Acknowledgements

The authors wish to acknowledge with gratitude the sponsorship of Cement Roadstone Holdings and the receipt of a publications grant from the Heritage Council. This greatly assisted the authors and the publisher in the production of this pictorial record of Ireland's bridge heritage. It is hoped that this publication will enable the general public to better appreciate this aspect of Ireland's built heritage.

The authors also gratefully acknowledge the assistance of the engineering staff and other personnel in the following:

Department of Civil, Structural & Environmental Engineering, Trinity College, Dublin; DoE Northern Ireland Roads Service; The Heritage Service of the Department of the Environment, Heritage & Local Government; Iarnród Éireann; The Institution of Engineers of Ireland; Local Authorities, Consultants and Contractors; Irish Cement; National Roads Authority; Northern Ireland Railways; School of Civil Engineering, Queen's University of Belfast; Science Library, Queen's University of Belfast; and Trinity College Library, Dublin.

Finally, the authors wish to thank all the members of the editorial and design team for their patience and professionalism in preparing the book for publication.❖

SUPPORTED BY THE HERITAGE COUNCIL

LE CUIDIÚ AN CHOMHAIRLE OIDHREACHTA

Preface

A community's social and commercial success is dependent in great measure on the existence of efficient and convenient transportation routes for goods and services. Bridges, by their very nature, form important links in such transportation routes and are an integral part of the built environment. Communities often grew up around important crossing points or bridges. *Ireland's Bridges* seeks to highlight the variety of this oft-unappreciated aspect of our built heritage.

The book is copiously illustrated, including many colour photographs. The authors have selected examples to illustrate the several arrangements and features of Irish bridge design and construction in a variety of settings. Most of the illustrations are accompanied by extended captions that provide a brief synopsis of the technical and other information relating to the specific bridge illustrated.

The first chapter provides an introduction to the historical development of Ireland's transportation networks and associated bridge stock, including enabling legislation, sources of funding and administrative arrangements. The second chapter examines the different bridge types and materials available to the designer and the basic ways in which bridges support the loads that they are required to carry. Bridges, whose elements are built largely of stone, metal or concrete, are treated in the chapters that follow. Finally, brief reference is made to recent developments occasioned by the expansion and improvement of Ireland's transportation infrastructure.

In a book on bridges, some use of the specialised terminology of structural engineering is unavoidable, but it is hoped that most of the terms will be understood from their context or from the explanations given in the glossary.

One of the most appealing aspects of viewing bridges is that one can normally enjoy them from afar, because of the unrestricted course of the river or ravine they span. It is the authors' hope that the book will help the reader to appreciate the contribution of bridges to the visual richness of the Irish landscape. ❖

Ronald Cox and Michael Gould
October 2003

CHAPTER ONE
HISTORY OF IRISH BRIDGES

History of Irish Bridges

The Bridge, even more than the Road, is a symbol of man's conquest of nature...
From the most primitive times it has been a dominant fact in the life of each community.
A bridge ruled the lines of traffic... Cities grew up around them, and castles were built to
command them. Battles were fought for their possession, and schemes of strategy were
based upon them... History – social, economic, and military –
clusters more thickly about bridges than about towns and citadels.
John Buchan, as quoted in *De la Mare* (1975)

community's social and commercial success is dependent in great measure on the existence of efficient and convenient transportation routes for goods and services. Bridges, by their very nature, form important links in such transportation routes and are an integral part of the built environment. As the writer Buchan observed, the strategic importance of bridges has resulted in battles being fought over them, castles being built to protect them and communities growing up around them.

At a time of unprecedented investment in infrastructure, including the completion of many new bridges built to exacting structural and aesthetic standards, it is appropriate to look back

ROAD AND RAIL BRIDGES,
NEWPORT, CO. MAYO.

LENNOX'S BRIDGE, COUNTY LEITRIM/DONEGAL BORDER

The old coastal route from Sligo to Bundoran crosses the Drowes River in County Donegal near the sea at what was probably a ford. Upriver, the eight -arch Lennox's Bridge is a typical early narrow stone structure with pedestrian refuges. The profiles of the arches are irregular, with two exhibiting a distinct point, in a manner reminiscent of the bridge at Killaloe, parts of which having been dated to around 1690.

SLANE BRIDGE, COUNTY MEATH

This multi-span masonry road bridge spanning the River Boyne near Slane Castle in County Meath is built in a mixture of styles. The pointed segmental arches on the downstream side indicate that the original parts of the structure could date from the mid 14th century. On the north-east side, two arches were added in 1776, when a weir and millrace were built. Such bridges, many of which are now protected by law, form part of our built heritage but present problems for today's heavy vehicular traffic and building a new bypass bridge is often the most economical and only solution.

at 1,200 years of bridge building in Ireland. From the earliest recorded bridge at Clonmacnoise over the River Shannon to the recently opened bridge carrying the M1 motorway across the Boyne valley to the west of Drogheda, this built heritage forms part of our richly varied landscape. Bridges are structures over which we frequently travel without being able to stop and appreciate their infinite variety.

It may be assumed that early bridge arrangements were based on certain simple structural forms observed in nature: the beam, for example as with a log felled across a stream; the arch, seen in some natural rock formations and the roofs of caves; while hanging vines suggested suspension as an alternative. A bridge may be defined as a structure spanning and providing passage over a road, waterway, railway or other obstacle. It has been estimated that there are around 25,000 stone arch bridges alone on the island of Ireland having at least one span of six feet (two metres) or more. Additional to these are bridges, viaducts and aqueducts of other design types and materials. The total Irish bridge stock is thus estimated to amount to some 30,000 structures of varying age, type and condition.

In this book, the authors have attempted to provide a photographic record of the variety of our bridge stock, the aim being to foster a greater appreciation of this important element of our built heritage. Given the large number of bridges, the authors have inevitably been forced to make choices as to which bridges should be included or excluded. Not all of those selected will be considered by every reader to be historically important or aesthetically pleasing, but each, the authors believe, has a place in the overall history of Irish bridges. To understand the reasons for the location of Irish bridges and the challenges facing bridge builders throughout the ages in crossing the various physical barriers to communication, it is necessary to understand the topography of the country.

Ireland consists of an undulating central plain of limestone, almost completely encircled by a coastal belt of high ground. This central plain is extensively covered with peat bog and glacial deposits of sand and clay and there are numerous lakes dotted over its surface. The River Shannon drains more than one fifth of the whole country. This, the longest river in

LOUISBURGH CLAPPER BRIDGE,
COUNTY MAYO

This clapper bridge (so-called from the flat slabs or 'clappers' used to span between the rubble piers) near Louisburgh in County Mayo is the largest in Ireland. Possibly dating from medieval times, the bridge has over thirty spans, the clappers or limestone slabs varying in length from 2ft 6in. to 5ft. The openings in the parapet walls allow the water to flow through unimpeded during times of flood. Such bridges were constructed where the water depth was small at times of normal flow and were often associated with an adjacent ford.

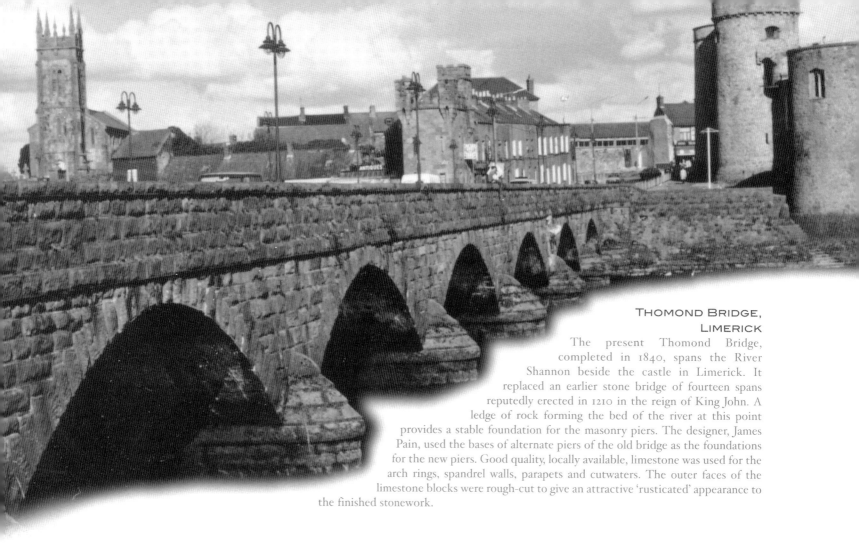

Ireland, flows south from its source to the north of Carrick-on-Shannon in County Leitrim to its estuary at Limerick and has always formed a significant barrier to east-west communications.

Proceeding clockwise around Ireland, to the north of the Shannon Basin, the River Erne flows westwards through the Fermanagh lake-land to Ballyshannon in County Donegal. Between the rugged mountains of Donegal and the Sperrins, the River Foyle flows northwards. Flowing northwards to Coleraine in County Londonderry, the Lower Bann drains Ireland's largest lake, Lough Neagh. Three rivers flow into the lough, the Main, the Upper Bann and the Ulster Blackwater.

The north-east corner of Ireland is a basaltic plateau furrowed by deep glens. To the south

the River Lagan enters the sea by Belfast Lough. The drumlin country of County Down leads in turn to the granite pile of the Mournes. Granite again comes to the surface in the Carlingford Mountains, but the greatest expanse of granite is in the Wicklow Mountains, running south from County Dublin to the borders of Counties Carlow and Wexford. North of this area, the limestone of the plain extends to the sea in the valleys of the River Boyne and River Liffey.

On the southern fringes of the central plain the older rocks outcrop as mountain ridges – as in the Galtee and Slieve Bloom Mountains. The main river systems of the Barrow, the Nore and the Suir drain a wide area and flow generally south-eastwards, combining to discharge into the sea at Waterford Harbour. These, together with the Slaney, which cuts south-eastwards through the hills to Wexford, and the Munster Blackwater, which flows eastwards in County Cork until turning south to form the border with County Waterford near Youghal, have been bridged in many places and this accounts for the greater concentration and variety of structures to be found in this part of Ireland.

CLADY BRIDGE, COUNTY TYRONE/DONEGAL BORDER

This narrow (12 ft) bridge spans the River Finn on the border between Counties Tyrone and Donegal. Clady Bridge has all the characteristics of medieval stone construction, having nine arches of differing size, each with a near semicircular profile. The piers are wide, with triangular cutwaters that are carried up to parapet level to form 11ft deep pedestrian refuges.

TERMONBARRY BRIDGE, COUNTY ROSCOMMON

At Termonbarry, the River Shannon is divided by an island into two channels, the bridge spanning the western channel being illustrated here. The 1840s masonry arch bridge replaced an earlier multi-span arch bridge whose foundations were found not to be suitable for underpinning. The navigation channel, originally spanned by an iron swivel bridge, is also clearly seen. A vertical lifting bridge was installed in the 1970s and a reinforced concrete deck with cantilevered footpaths was superimposed over the masonry bridge in 1993. This provided the necessary width for the main road between the county towns of Longford and Roscommon.

The south and south-west region is mainly a system of east and west foldings of old red sandstone. Limestone generally occupies the valley bottoms between the upland folds and in places the rivers have cut gorges through the ridges. Proceeding westwards, the ridges pile up in mountains, reaching their maximum height in County Kerry.

As indicated on the map, the rivers of Ireland, apart from the Shannon, are generally small. However, in times of high rainfall, many rivers flood, damaging, and in severe circumstances, totally destroying bridges, particularly those of light construction. To regulate the flow and alleviate flooding of adjacent

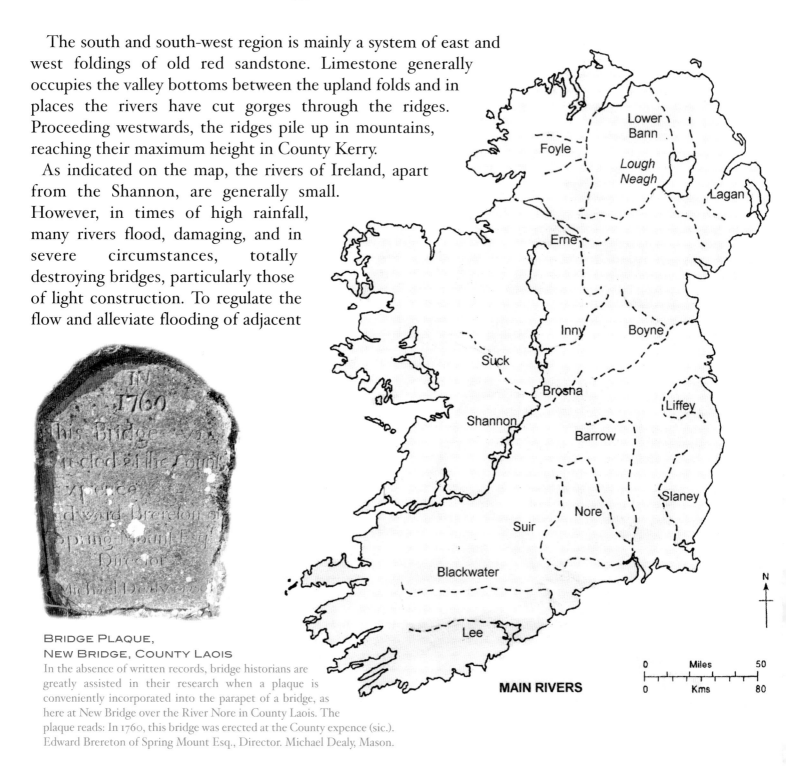

**BRIDGE PLAQUE,
NEW BRIDGE, COUNTY LAOIS**

In the absence of written records, bridge historians are greatly assisted in their research when a plaque is conveniently incorporated into the parapet of a bridge, as here at New Bridge over the River Nore in County Laois. The plaque reads: In 1760, this bridge was erected at the County expence (sic.). Edward Brereton of Spring Mount Esq., Director. Michael Dealy, Mason.

CARRICK-A-REDE ROPE BRIDGE, COUNTY ANTRIM

A link allowing fishermen access to the Carrick-a-Rede rock near the Giant's Causeway in County Antrim has existed for two hundred years. By Victorian times, the bridge had been discovered by tourists visiting the nearby causeway and the bridge has been an attraction ever since. The deck is laid directly onto the suspension cables, the handrails having no structural function and many have refused to cross the resulting swaying structure. Recent health and safety legislation has raised doubts about the continued use of the bridge, which is now replaced annually and is only open during the summer months. A concerted effort has been made to stiffen the structure to eliminate sway.

lands, many of the river systems have been the subject of arterial drainage schemes, and many old stone bridges have had concrete protective skirts placed around the bases of their piers and abutments.

The extensive system of routes that existed in ancient Ireland evolved over many centuries into our present network of roads. River crossings were very important in determining the line of any road. Before the construction of bridges, the crossing of wide rivers was accomplished at fords, by means of stepping-stones at shallow places, or by ferry. The Irish name for Dublin, 'Baile Atha Cliath', means the 'town of the hurdle ford'; that for Belfast, 'Baile Feirste' has been given in one translation as 'the place of the sand-bar', thought to refer to a ford on the River Lagan. In a few places so-called clapper bridges were used in association with fords, a notable example being that located to the west of Louisburgh in County Mayo (see p.5).

Castlecomer Bridge, County Kilkenny

Following the flood of 1763, the Commissioners for Inland Navigation were charged with the task of replacing or repairing a number of bridges on the River Nore and its main tributaries. Here at Castlecomer in County Kilkenny, George Smith was commissioned to carry out major repairs to the bridge over the Dinin River. Like Green's Bridge in Kilkenny, he rebuilt it in the Palladian style, adding niches over the cutwaters. The bridge was further repaired in 1992 and a picnicking area established nearby on the banks of the river.

FATHER MATTHEW BRIDGE, DUBLIN

King John signed a charter in 1215 for the building of the first bridge of any substance at or near the site of the original 'atha cliath' or 'ford of hurdles', from which Dublin gets its Irish name. The present Father Matthew Bridge was designed and built by George Knowles, who had been the contractor for the nearby O'Donovan Rossa Bridge, designed by James Savage. The balustraded parapets of this pair of Liffey bridges are continued along the quaysides and make a notable contribution to the architectural heritage of this area of the city.

It is not clear when the first formal bridges were built in Ireland. The ancient Irish smith-god Gonbniu was noted as a builder of bridges. While this may be seen as implying some form of metal bridge, other records tell of wicker bridges and mention examples being built and destroyed in very short time intervals. Further, the substantial remains of a timber trestle bridge spanning the Shannon at Clonmacnoise in County Offaly have been carbon-dated to 804 A.D. It would thus seem safe to assume that early bridges in Ireland were primarily built of timber, the input of the blacksmith being limited to the making of tools, nails and straps for such bridges.

CLONMACNOISE BRIDGE, COUNTY OFFALY

Discovered in 1994 by two divers, the Clonmacnoise bridge in County Offaly is the oldest identifiable bridge ever discovered in Ireland. Sufficient remains of the bridge have been found to indicate how it may have been constructed. Erected in 804 A.D., and seen here in a model reconstruction, the bridge was up to 15ft in width and spanned 390ft across the River Shannon. Longitudinal beams of oak were inserted into the tops of vertical posts by way of a plain bridle-joint, in order to create a frame onto which transverse timbers were fitted using a halved lap joint.

TULNASHANE BRIDGE, COUNTY DONEGAL

Tulnashane Bridge over the River Derg to the north of Pettigo in County Donegal was one of a number of bridges on minor cross-border roads that were cratered as a security measure during the Troubles. Since the Good Friday Agreement, all of those found to be still impassable have been replaced. The bridge was a two-span stone arch structure with spans of 18/21 ft on the road from Killeter to Pettigo via Legvin. In 1995, it was reinstated in concrete featured to resemble a stone arch ring with natural stone parapets and using the existing stone foundations.

CAST-IRON SWIVEL BRIDGE, SHANNONBRIDGE, COUNTY OFFALY

Removal of the cast-iron swivel bridge designed by Robert Mallet and erected 1843 over the navigation channel at Shannonbridge in County Offaly.
It was replaced in the 1980s with a simple reinforced concrete fixed span.

An alternative to a timber bridge was the wicker bridge, and there are records of such bridges being thrown across rivers in the 12th century. Early references to wicker bridges are, however, imprecise. It is not clear if these refer to wicker baskets filled with stone to provide foundations for short-span timber beams, or some form of interlaced arch of branches. Such structures rarely survived severe winter floods and had to be frequently repaired or replaced. A present-day example of a temporary bridge that is taken down for the winter months is the Carrick-a-Rede rope suspension footbridge in County Antrim (see p.9).

As the skills of carpenters improved, so more substantial timber bridges were erected and became widely distributed along the developing trade routes. Ireland was then rich in timber and local carpenters would have found it an easy material to obtain and work with. The services of skilled stonemasons would not have been so easily procured.

Timber-decked bridges spanning between stone abutments lasted until the 20th century, the timber bridge at Wexford not being replaced until as late as 1959. However, a study of the surviving records show that such bridges needed almost annual maintenance. The use of timber is suggested in the following extract from a poem published in 1899 and one of few that refer to the actual structural form of the bridge, in this case beams:

The gladdening sunbeams through the trees,
the bridges beams adorn,
on every side the mayflower grow,
and the cuckoo birds are born,
our land has not, a sweeter spot,
than the Carrick Bridge at morn.

RINGSEND BRIDGE, DUBLIN

The old road from Dublin to Ringsend (formerly a fishing village) crosses the tidal River Dodder by a single-span stone bridge erected in 1812 to replace an earlier structure carried away by a flood in 1802. The arch has an elliptical profile and the edges are chamfered to aid the passage of floodwaters. The abutments are continued downwards as a curve to form a paved riverbed. Both these elements of the design ensure good hydraulic flow conditions. As with a small number of bridges in other parts of the country, the spandrel walls are formed by a continuation of the voussoir stones in the arch ring.

SARSFIELD BRIDGE, LIMERICK

Wellesley (now Sarsfield) Bridge spanning the River Shannon at Limerick was designed by Alexander Nimmo and completed by John Grantham in 1835. It is said that Nimmo was greatly influenced by Jean Rodolphe Perronet's design for the Pont Neuilly in Paris. The five ashlar limestone arches of the main bridge are each of 70ft span with a rise of only 8ft 6in. In order to aid the flow in the river, the height above the waterline at which each arch springs reduces from the face of the arch to the bridge centreline. The tops of the cutwaters are carved in the shape of seashells. The pierced balustrades were rebuilt in 1975 to commemorate European Architectural Heritage Year.

LEIGHLINBRIDGE, COUNTY CARLOW

The crossing of the River Barrow at Leighlinbridge in County Carlow has been important since the 10th century. The first stone bridge to be built on the site was erected around 1320 and it seems likely that the bridge was rebuilt in the mid 17th century and widened in 1789. As many old bridges are quite narrow, it is not always possible to accommodate both vehicular traffic and pedestrians with safety. In 1976, a cantilevered reinforced concrete footpath was added to the upstream face. Since 1986, the Carlow to Kilkenny road has bypassed the village and the bridge has been allowed to grow old gracefully.

The Normans used their mastery of building in stone to erect arch bridges. Examples may be found at Boyle in County Roscommon (Abbeytown Bridge) and on a private estate near Portlaw in County Waterford (King John's Bridge). Routes, such as that between Dublin and Waterford, attracted considerable attention and some notable stone bridges were constructed at strategic river crossing points, for example at Leighlinbridge in County Carlow. However, as the Anglo-Norman dominance in Ireland declined after 1350, there was a break-up of the manorial system, this in turn leading to a decline in the maintenance of roads and bridges and travel became difficult and dangerous.

The Highway Act (1613-15), for the 'repairing and amending of highways and cashes and cutting and clearing of paces' brought to Ireland the statute labour system, which had operated in England from 1555. Each year every parish elected a Surveyor and an Orderer. The Surveyor determined six days in early summer for the repair of the parish roads. Every farmer was required to send two able men with a team and tools to work for eight hours. Each cottager had to present himself for work. Everyone, including the Surveyor, was liable to fines for default in the performance of these duties. Responsibility for statute labour was later shifted from the parishes to the counties by an amendment of the Highway Act. In 1634, an Act 'concerning the repairing and amending of bridges, causeys and toghers in the high-ways' empowered the Grand Jury to levy rates for this purpose. The statute labour system continued until 1765.

In 1710, the Grand Jury system, which had originated in Norman times, was established in Ireland. The members of the Grand Juries were mainly wealthy landowners selected by the Sheriff of the County. Meeting twice each year before the Assizes, they could receive presentments from each Barony in the county for works, which could not be undertaken by statute labour. If formally approved by a Judge of the Assizes, rates would be levied and work could then proceed. In 1739, additional powers were given to acquire land for road building.

BRIDGE COMPETITION DESIGN, 1862

A competition to find the most appropriate and acceptable design for a structure that will have a major impact on a community is not a new phenomenon. In 1862, a design by Richard Turner and George Page for a single arch iron bridge won first place in a competition to replace Sackville (later O'Connell) Bridge in Dublin. However, due to cost and potential maintenance implications, iron was not finally selected and the present masonry arch bridge was erected. Iron structures, in particular bridges, have been considered by many to possess little architectural merit, but then it is said, *"beauty is in the eye of the beholder"*.

**LEVITSTOWN LIFTING BRIDGE,
COUNTY KILDARE**
An unusual 'guillotine' vertical lifting bridge at Levitstown on the Barrow Navigation in County Kildare. The bridge provides access across the navigation for local traffic and can be raised by hand when required to allow passage of water-borne traffic.

**MAYSFIELD LIFTINGBRIDGE,
BELFAST**
A modern application of the old drawbridge principle, this twin-arm lifting bridge, providing access to the Maysfield yacht marina at Belfast, was completed in 1994 to a design by Shepheard Epstein & Hunter of London.

In 1765 the Grand Jury was given powers to present for any road works, including associated bridges. Many of the Grand Jury records were lost during the Civil War and, as a result, the dating of bridges is difficult. In some instances, however, bridge plaques can provide useful information.

The first Turnpike Act in Ireland was enacted in 1727. Trusts were appointed by Parliament, each to manage a defined length of road while tolls could be collected from the users to defray the cost. Under this Act, it was stipulated that roads had to have a minimum width of 12ft. Some years later, a further Act raised this to 14ft and extended the directive to include bridges. It is reckoned that the introduction of this legislation was one of the main reasons for the eventual removal or rebuilding of many of the narrow medieval bridges. Eventually some eighty similar local acts were passed covering about 1,500 miles of road. However, the

turnpikes could not compete with the railways and the last was abolished in 1857. The collection of tolls was also a common feature of bridges at major river crossings and bridge-masters were on occasions appointed to look after the repair and maintenance of the bridge.

The introduction of mail coaches in 1789 gave a fresh impetus to road planning and construction in Ireland. The passing of the Act of 1805 'to amend the laws for improving and keeping in repair the post roads in Ireland...' brought a new radical approach to road building and the introduction of the first geometric design standards. The subject of standards for road works received much attention in France from about 1780 onwards. The school of bridges and highways (the École de Ponts et Chausées), founded in Paris in 1747, pioneered

BRIDGE PLAQUE, SHAW'S BRIDGE & LOCK, ROYAL CANAL

The building of the Grand and Royal canals required the construction of many bridges to carry roads over the navigations. Such bridges were usually of a standard design along any stretch of canal built under the supervision of a particular engineer. The bridges frequently have a plaque on the parapet wall positioned so that it may be read from the waterway. This plaque, on the Royal Canal, is typical and contains the date of erection, the name of the bridge, and the name of the engineer '1795, Shaw's Bridge & Lock, R.Evans, Eng.'

much of the scientific road and bridge building practices at this period, and this had an important influence on road engineering throughout Western Europe.

In a great many cases, more than one bridge structure has existed for successive periods at any given location, the first bridge often being built at the site of a ford. Information on such earlier bridges is difficult to come by, but the bridges in the town of Enniskillen in County Fermanagh may serve as an example of the typical development seen over the years.

The fortified town of Enniskillen, on an island between Upper and Lower Lough Erne, was originally approached from the direction of Belfast by a 12ft wide timber drawbridge and

ROSE GARDEN FOOTBRIDGE,
BOTANIC GARDENS, DUBLIN

This small-span functional Pratt truss footbridge across the River Tolka provides access to the Rose Garden at the Botanic Gardens in Dublin. The trusses are formed of lengths of steel L-section, and are strengthened to resist maximum bending at mid-span by the addition of extra diagonal elements.

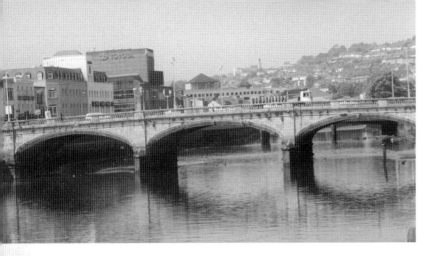

St Patrick's Bridge, Cork

Following heavy flooding in the River Lee in November 1853, when the masonry bridge, opened in 1789, collapsed with the loss of twenty lives, Sir John Benson, the Cork City Engineer and Architect, drew up plans for a new bridge over the north channel of the river at this end of Patrick Street. Built by Joshua Hargrave, the present St Patrick's Bridge, with its pierced balustrades, has three arches with an elliptical or three-centred profile, the arch rings being stepped back to assist water flow. The foundations were taken down to 14ft below low water ordinary spring tides and the piers were formed of caissons filled with concrete and reinforced with transverse iron bars.

Westland Row Rail Bridge, Dublin

This engraving from the pages of The Engineer of 1880 depicts the decorative iron railway bridge spanning Westland Row in Dublin. Work can be seen proceeding on the western façade of the railway station in preparation for the opening of the link across the river to Connolly station. Dublin did not appear to have a problem with motorised road traffic in those days, even the trams being horse-drawn.

from the direction of Donegal by another, probably even narrower bridge. Defensive works for the protection of this western crossing still exist. The first stone bridge to the west of the town, possibly dating from 1698, had at least eight arches. It is said to have been identical to the bridge at Ballyshannon - a not unlikely occurrence, given that the stonemasons themselves had a great influence on bridge design. Old 14th century bridges, like that at Trim in County Meath, have arches of a span approximately twice the thickness of the intervening piers. These small span multi-arch bridges presented an obstruction to river flow, so in 1773, a three-arch stone replacement was built. In turn, a drainage scheme in the Erne catchment in County Fermanagh led to the three-arch bridge being replaced by the present twin three-centered arch bridge, on which there is an inscription that reads 'ERNE BRIDGE 1885'.

The Liffey Rail Viaduct forming part of the 'Loop Line' was completed in 1891 and connects Westland Row (now Pearse) station with Amiens Street (now Connolly) station in Dublin. It consists of a three-span bridge of twin wrought-iron latticed girders supported on pairs of cylindrical cast-iron caissons sunk to rock and in-filled with concrete. The designer was John Chaloner Smith and the structural ironwork was supplied and erected by William Arrol of Glasgow. Immediately upstream of the viaduct is a reinforced concrete road bridge, opened in 1932 to replace an earlier opening swing bridge. Butt Bridge was designed by Joseph Mallagh (Chief Engineer of Dublin Port) and Professor Pierce Purcell of University College Dublin. Construction was by Gray's Ferro-Concrete (Ireland) Ltd.

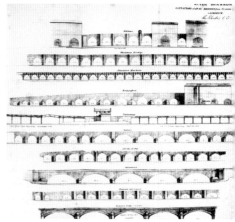

SHANNON BRIDGES SURVEY

Commissioners for the River Shannon Navigation were appointed in 1831, Thomas Rhodes being appointed as their engineer to carry out a survey of the navigation. He prepared elevations of all the bridges across the river from its source in Lough Allen in County Leitrim to Limerick. The drawings, which accompanied his reports, are a valuable record of the bridges, as they existed at that time. The old Thomond Bridge at Limerick is shown, as is the remarkable medieval bridge at Athlone. These interfered with the flow of the river and were replaced in the subsequent combined drainage and navigation scheme undertaken in the 1840s.

East Bridge in County Fermanagh was replaced in 1688 in stone, but was only 5ft wide. This bridge was widened in 1832, the pedestrian refuges in the parapet, a feature of many old narrow bridges, being removed (apparently, these had become haunts for beggars). A further widening was undertaken around 1894. As the major drainage works had previously taken place in the main river channel in the vicinity of the West Bridge, there was no requirement

SALMON WEIR BRIDGE, GALWAY

The architect, Vitruvius Morrison, designed a classical bridge in ashlar limestone to span the River Corrib near the famous salmon weirs in Galway City. It is said that the bridge was located at this point to provide a convenient route from the courthouse on one side of the river to the jail on the other! It is difficult to appreciate the original appearance of the bridge due to the number of piped services fixed to the spandrel walls (particularly on the downstream side). The arch soffits have been sprayed with concrete and anti-scour skirts provided around the bases of the piers.

LISTOWEL BRIDGE, COUNTY KERRY

Between 1823 and 1839, the government engineer, Richard Griffith, opened up lines of communication by building roads and several major bridges in the south-west of Ireland. The bridge pictured here crosses the River Feale to the south of Listowel in County Kerry and was completed in 1829. The five segmental arches are each of 53ft span and 11ft 9in. rise. The simple, but robust, design was carried out in fine quality ashlar limestone, relieved by an archivolt, projecting string course and parapet cap stones. Rectangular section pilasters are carried upwards to the parapets from the tops of the pointed cutwaters.

to remove the old bridge, which is contained within the present structure. It is believed that a number of the original arches still exist under the road as a result of bank infilling for building. The widened bridge has allowed for a realignment of the road. The successive widening of the eastern bridge represents an example of what has happened on many sites throughout Ireland that have not been subject to replacement. This pattern of successive bridge replacements or widening has generally been replicated throughout the country.

The proportions, structural efficacy and architectural and aesthetic merit of bridges varied considerably. City administrations were always more conscious of the aesthetics of bridges and were able to raise money from the traders and citizens to finance bridges of quality, often engaging leading architects to undertake the design and supervision of the work, an example of a competition for a bridge design being that for O'Connell Bridge in Dublin. Cities, such as Dublin, Belfast and Cork generally boast the finest of our bridges, but notable bridges have also been constructed in other urban areas, such as Limerick and Galway; while some fine examples are to be found in rural areas

EGYPTIAN ARCH, COUNTY DOWN

A favourite of postcard publishers, the Egyptian Arch was built in 1851 by the Dublin & Belfast Junction Railway to take their line over the Newry to Camlough Road. Designed by Sir John Macneill, it reflected a contempory interest in things Egyptian. The contractor for the arch was William Dargan. Since the card (from which this illustration was taken) passed through the post in 1906, the parapet has been reduced in height and the view has been affected by the Newry bypass.

spanning the major river systems. In earlier times, such bridges were on occasions financed by local landed gentry or religious orders, but more often than not, a local tax or rate was levied on the population directly benefiting from the work. In other instances, central government provided the resources to build roads and bridges to open up the more remote areas of the country, often in order to gain faster access for military and other government personnel when required.

Canal building in Ireland took place mainly between 1730 and 1860. Although small in span, canal bridges are also an important element of our built heritage, providing a visually pleasing backdrop to many a stretch of canal. Many have plaques providing information as to the date of erection and the name of the canal engineer. Occasionally, lifting bridges have been installed across the canal as an alternative to a fixed structure. The main lines of canal (as shown on the map on p.24) are carried in places over rivers by means of beautifully executed stone aqueducts.

TERRYHOOGAN AQUEDUCT, COUNTY DOWN

The stone aqueduct at Terryhoogan may be the oldest such structure still extant. The Newry Canal, completed in 1741, and the first summit level canal in Britain or Ireland, was not without its problems. To improve the water supply, Acheson Jackson proposed in 1750 an open channel from the Cusher River at Tandragee in County Armagh to the summit level of the canal. It seems that Terryhoogan aqueduct dates from this time. The narrow 6ft width of the ten-arch stone structure suggests that the water was conveyed over it in a wooden trough.

BARROW AQUEDUCT, COUNTY KILDARE

This aqueduct, designed by Hamilton Killaly, was built between 1827 and 1831 to carry the Barrow Line of the Grand Canal over the River Barrow near Monasterevan in County Kildare. The voissoirs in the arch rings of the three 41ft 6in. spans are rusticated ashlar limestone and the garlanded decoration over each river pier gives the aqueduct an attractive overall appearance.

Canals are of one of two types. Those that follow existing rivers, with short artificial cuts and locks to bypass bends, shallows or waterfalls, are referred to as 'navigations'. Totally artificial cuts, which generally go from one river catchment to the next, are referred to as 'summit' or 'still-water' canals. These require the provision of an artificial water supply. The first modern summit canal in either Britain or Ireland was the Newry Canal (completed 1741). Other lines followed, including the east-west lines of the Grand Canal (with a branch southwards to the River Barrow Navigation) and the Royal Canal connecting Dublin with the River Shannon. Belfast was soon connected to Lough Neagh by way of the River Lagan. Other lines included the Ulster and Ballinamore-Ballyconnell Canals and the Lower Bann and Shannon Navigations, this latter being a major undertaking.

An aqueduct is built to carry an open watercourse across an obstruction (although the term is now sometimes used for closed pipes flowing under the action of gravity). In the

MAIN LINES OF CANAL

- - - Open
.... Closed

context of inland navigations, an aqueduct carries a river over the canal; the canal over some obstruction without the need for locks or convey feed water into the canal. Due to the nature of Ireland's topography and river systems, it has been found necessary to construct aqueducts at only a few locations.

The greatest weakness of the 1805 Act relating to road construction was that the implementation of the road plans was left in the hands of the Grand Juries. Central government had no powers to compel the Grand Juries to carry out the work and had no authority to give grants for the schemes. This latter defect was made good to some extent in 1822, when Parliament was empowered to make grants to the Grand Juries for the formation of specific roads and bridges. This led to a period during which government engineers, such as Richard Griffith, Alexander Nimmo, and John Killaly supervised the building of many miles of road and numbers of substantial masonry bridges.

The Irish Board of Works was established in 1831; its functions included the management of the funds for road grants and loans. The Board made a major contribution to the development and repair of the principal roads, streets and bridges over the ensuing years. One of the first contracts to be undertaken by the Commissioners of Public Works for Ireland was the reconstruction of the County Antrim coast road to a design by William Bald. This road

KILCUMMER RAIL VIADUCT,
COUNTY CORK

The Great Southern & Western Railway branch from Mallow to Fermoy was carried over the valley of the Awbeg River to the west of Fermoy on the ten-span Kilcummer viaduct approximately 56ft above ground. The single track was supported on pairs of latticed girders set 5ft 3in. apart 'centre to centre' and spanning between slender masonry piers. The spans are 45ft with a main river span of 51ft. The engineer was William le Fanu (who took the photograph shortly after the viaduct was completed in 1860) and the contractor was the famous William Dargan.

was completed in sections over several years, the first part across Cushleake Mountain containing a number of small bridges. Each has its name, date and an OS bench mark, cut into the parapet. Construction on the Antrim coastal route also saw the first use in Ireland of gunpowder, used to collapse the seaward face of the cliffs to form a platform on which the road was then constructed.

In 1836, the Grand Juries took over responsibility for the construction and maintenance of all public roads and bridges and the Lord Lieutenant was empowered to appoint a Surveyor for each county. A number of these county surveyors combined the role of engineer with that of architect, Sir Charles Benson in Cork, for example, not only designing St Patrick's Bridge over the River Lee, but also a number of the public buildings in that city.

Bridges erected by wealthy landowners on private estates and demesnes form another intriguing group of heritage structures. There is a surprising variety of bridge types, some, like the suspension bridge at Birr Castle (c.1826) and the cast-iron bridge at Oak Park near Carlow (1818) being of international significance.

BALBRIGGAN RAIL VIADUCT, COUNTY DUBLIN

The Dublin to Drogheda section of the mainline from Dublin to Belfast was opened in 1844. At Balbriggan in County Dublin, the contractor, William Dargan, built an eleven-arch viaduct to carry the double-track railway over four roads and a small river. A variety of materials were used in the building of the viaduct. The outer arch rings and spandrel walls are of limestone, whereas the engineer, Sir John Macneill, decided on the use of brick for the inner arch rings. Brick was also used for the internal diaphragm walls. Footpaths each side of the viaduct are supported on cast-iron arches spanning between the piers.

The coming of the railways after 1830 presented engineers with the challenge of spanning the major rivers. Rail bridges and viaducts constitute a lasting memorial to the ingenuity and determination of the 19th century engineers, although many of these structures have been altered or, in some cases, replaced in recent times. Where a railway route needed to cross a valley or other large depression, the railway engineers, wishing to limit the slope (or 'gradient') up and down which the train had to pass, used a succession of masonry arches spanning between solid masonry piers of varying height. Such viaducts are immensely strong and built to last. Later, when iron became more available, it was used for both railway viaducts and single-span bridges over the wider rivers.

The first railway to be opened in Ireland ran the eight miles from Dublin to Kingstown (now Dun Laoghaire). Designed

MAP OF MAIN RAILWAYS

largely by Charles Vignoles, it was constructed by one of the major contractors of the day, William Dargan, and was opened in 1834. The building of the Ulster Railway from Belfast to Armagh soon followed. These lines used different gauges (the distance between the running rails) and a Gauge Act was eventually passed by Parliament to settle the issue, which lead to the compromise Irish gauge of 5ft 3in. Although a Government Commission was established in 1836 to plan a national railway network, building was left to the private sector. Towards the end of the 19th century, some government assistance was provided for the construction of railways or tramways (often to a narrow gauge of 3ft) in the more remote areas of the country. Much of Ireland's network was single track and large sections were not remunerative; wholesale closures in the 20th century of what was once a nationwide system followed, with the bridges sometimes being removed. The main lines of railway are indicated on the map. (Rail bridges are classed as 'under' or 'over', these terms relating to the support of the permanent way, thus an under-bridge carries the running track.) With the completion of the railways, the basic transport infrastructure in Ireland was in place. However, the introduction of motor vehicles led to an expansion in the work of road improvement.

BLACKWATER BRIDGE,
COUNTY CLARE

Provision of a navigable headrace and tailrace at the Ardnacrusha hydroelectric works on the River Shannon in County Clare (built 1925-29) necessitated the construction of four concrete bridges with a clearance of 12ft to allow for the passage of boats. Two of these were three-pin single span arches whilst two, including the Blackwater Bridge depicted here, consist of four parallel beams. These extend from the abutments on each bank to the river piers and then cantilever out a further 26ft 6in. A simply supported mid-section completes the central span of 112ft. The beams, which vary in depth from 6ft 3in to 14ft 3in, rest on steel bearings rather than being cast contiguous with the abutments. All the bridges were designed in Germany by engineers from the contractors Siemens Schukert.

As the 19th century drew to a close, the Local Government (Ireland) Act of 1898 placed local government on a representative basis, transferring to elected Councils such Grand Jury business that was not connected with the administration of justice. The 1634 Act for repairing and amending bridges had remained in force until

SOLITUDE PARK, COUNTY DOWN

Completed in 1978, this 48m long asymmetric cable-stayed footbridge at Banbridge in County Down was erected by Clyde Structural Steel Co. Ltd. It forms part of Solitude Park, a linear riverside park developed by Enterprise Ulster (a body intended to provide work experience and training to construction workers) for Banbridge District Council. By locating the support tower back from the riverbank, the designer, Dr Doran & Partners, avoided difficult foundation works within the Upper Bann River.

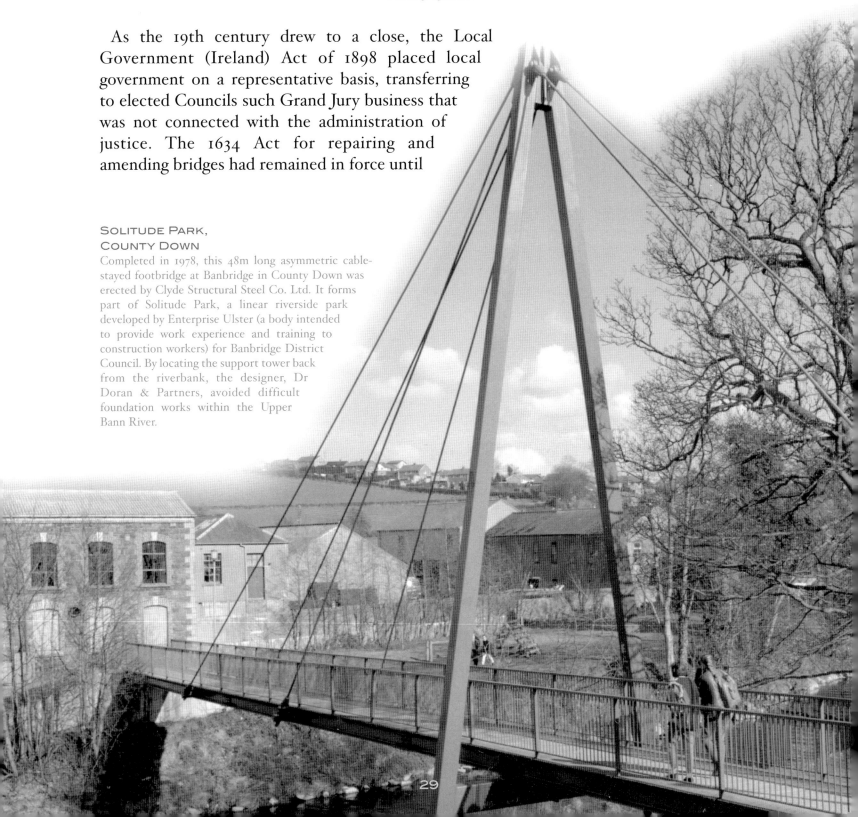

This five-span reinforced concrete road bridge spanning the Abbey River in Limerick was designed by James Joseph Roughan in association with the Yorkshire Hennbique Construction Company, who constructed the bridge. The piers and abutments are supported on reinforced concrete 'needle' piles and the two central river piers are cross-braced to add stability to the structure. The bridge deck rises from either side to a higher central span, designed to provide adequate headroom for navigation. The bridge was opened in 1931 and named in honour of a former bishop of Limerick, Edward O'Dwyer.

the Grand Juries were abolished by the 1898 Act. The Act brought about a major change in the organisation and management of roads and other local services. County Councils, assisted by Rural and Urban District Councils, took over the functions of the Grand Juries. Under the grand jury system, mail coach routes and some important bridges could be declared as 'county at large' works paid for on a countywide bases, all other works being charged to the relevant Barony. The County Councils were now able to declare a greater proportion of their roads as main roads, but only half of the cost of maintenance of such roads was borne by the county, all other work being charged to the district through which the road passed.

In 1909, the Development & Road Improvements Act imposed special taxes on motorists; the money raised was used to establish a Road Fund from which grants were distributed for road improvement works. The sums raised were, however, totally inadequate and as a result, the road network was generally in a poor condition. Following the Treaty in 1922, the future development and improvement of Ireland's road network was placed in the hands of the road authorities of the separate jurisdictions, with a consequential divergence in transport policy. The Dublin government set about the task of repairing the bridges damaged during the Civil War, setting aside a sizeable sum of money for this purpose. The Stormont administration adopted a policy of using the entire road fund for road works. The quality of roads north of the border improved steadily as a consequence with, for example, concrete surfaces being first laid during the 1930s.

By the end of the 1920s, at the time of the construction of the Shannon Scheme to harness the power of the river to generate electricity, the use of reinforced concrete was well developed. The three reinforced concrete bridges spanning the intake canal to the hydroelectric works at Ardnacrusha in County Clare, are fine examples of the period and have lasted well.

In 1925, a new Act of the Irish Free State ushered in a decade during which the extent of bridge building and repair, on both road and rail routes, proved unprecedented. In 1926, Rural District Councils were disbanded in the Republic, although they continued to exist in Northern Ireland until 1973. This work of improvement continued in the Irish Free State up to WWII as funds were made available. During this time 365 bridges were improved or replaced and 112 new bridges erected, mostly of small span. As commercial vehicle weights increased, so load restrictions had to be placed on certain bridges. In 1962-63, the Minister for Local Government in the Republic, designated 1,500 miles of the more important trunk and link roads as arterial routes and provided grants for developing these principal routes.

ANNAGOLA BRIDGE, COUNTY ARMAGH

The damaged three-span stone arch bridge was removed in the 1980s as part of the Ulster Blackwater drainage scheme, thus the replacement was commissioned by the Northern Ireland Rivers Agency. The Annagola Bridge at Middletown in County Armagh, opened in 1997, is a blend of traditional and modern. The single 26m span was built using pre-cast pre-stressed Y-beams. The visible stonework is intended to blend this new material with the existing stonework of the Ulster Canal, which lies just beyond. Although abandoned since 1931, a study is presently in hand to ascertain if the canal can be reopened, but it is intended to retain as much as possible of the remaining stonework. Design was by W D R & R T Taggart and the contractor was Deane Public Works Ltd.

Some of these would later be upgraded to dual-carriageway or motorway standard.

The upsurge in the Troubles north of the border from 1956 resulted in some bridges being attacked and damaged. Later, some bridges spanning the border on unapproved roads were deliberately cratered but, with the return of more peaceful conditions, all have now been reinstated, often using modern materials.

Possibly the most significant engineering work to affect a large proportion of multi-span stone bridges spanning the major river systems has been that of arterial drainage. Each of the main rivers and its associated catchment areas was designated as a drainage area. Much of the work carried out under arterial drainage Acts was designed to prevent, or at least limit, the annual flooding of lands lying adjacent to the main river channels. The channels were generally straightened and deepened and, as a result, many bridges had to be strengthened or underpinned, or replaced. It is reckoned that arterial drainage schemes have been associated with over 2,000 miles of river channel, affecting over 6,000 bridges.

There are currently three principal agencies that have responsibility for the bridge stock in the Republic of Ireland. Bridges on regional roads are maintained by the relevant Local Authorities, with general policy being dictated by central government, in particular the Department of the Environment, Heritage & Local Government. Bridges on primary roads, including motorways, are the responsibility of the National Roads Authority (NRA). The NRA has in place a bridge management system known as EIRSPAN under which they are able to assess the condition of major road bridges. Iarnród Éireann (Irish Rail) is responsible for a large number of under- and over-bridges, the vast majority being of masonry construction. The low headroom provided by some of the original arched over-bridges has necessitated their replacement for operational reasons. The replacements are generally of flat soffit concrete and/or steel construction.

RATHCOOLE FOOTBRIDGE,
COUNTY DUBLIN
A cable-stayed footbridge crossing the N7 at Rathcoole to the west of Dublin. The 40m main span is constructed of parallel steel plate girders with a steel half through deck, whilst the 19m high A-frame pylon is made up from hollow steel tubing. The main span is supported by two pairs of 45mm diameter spiral strand stay cables, whilst a single pair of 66mm cables stabilise the pylon and are taken back to the foundations. Design was by Carl Bro Ireland and the contractor was Clonmel Enterprises. The steelwork was supplied by Thompson Engineering.

In Northern Ireland, the first stretch of motorway was opened in 1968 between Belfast and Lisburn. An ambitious network was proposed and some 200 new bridges were built. However rising oil prices led to a reappraisal of motorway construction, with a number of routes where work had not started later being abandoned. In 1973, local government reorganisation passed the control of all public roads to the Ministry of Development, subsequently the Roads Service of the Department of the Environment for Northern Ireland and now of the Department for Regional Development. The Road Fund was abolished in 1973 and road works are currently funded directly by central government.

The realignment of main roads and the provision of bypasses around major towns lying along the routes, have resulted in a number of our historic bridges being relieved of heavy traffic with the provision of new separate and generally parallel structures. Membership of the European Union has affected the axle weights of heavy goods vehicles permitted on the roads and bridges. These have had to be assessed as to their suitability to carry these loads, with a number being

strengthened as a result. The Irish government has made considerable use of the regional infrastructural funding available to upgrade the road network, including the provision of long stretches of dual carriageway and motorways radiating from Dublin. This has required the construction of a number of modern bridges in concrete and steel.

The reorganisation and improvement of facilities for both private and public transportation in Dublin, Belfast and other major population centres, led to an upsurge in construction of new dedicated road networks and standard and light railways. These often require new bridges or the strengthening of existing structures. Growing leisure time has resulted in projects reopening many kilometres of canal and the provision of long-distance cycle ways. The reconstruction of the Shannon-Erne Waterway involved the building of a number of concrete bridges faced with local stone in the style of the original canal bridges. Such schemes are supported by both governments, Aghalane Bridge on the County Fermanagh/Cavan border, for example, being declared open jointly by Lord Dubs and Noel Dempsey, TD, in 1999. This structure was renamed the Senator George Mitchell Peace Bridge. Dedicated combined pedestrian/cycle ways have an added advantage in improved safety, as they are separated from vehicular traffic. Some structures on such routes reflect older design forms, such as the drawbridge at the Maysfield Leisure Centre in Belfast.

There has been a growing appreciation and understanding of the impact of bridges on the environment and a marked improvement in bridge aesthetics, notably the treatment of surfaces, the application of the arch form and variations of the cable-stayed design concept. ❖

M50/N2 MOTORWAY INTERCHANGE,
COUNTY DUBLIN
Effective false arch detailing used to mask the simple concrete beam and slab design of this bridge at the M50/N2 motorway interchange to the west of Dublin. Design was by Campbell, Conroy, Hickey, Rooney Associates and construction by P.J. Walls.

BIRR CASTLE SUSPENSION BRIDGE
COUNTY OFFALY

This is the earliest wire suspension bridge in Ireland. The footbridge, spanning 44ft
across the Camcor River in the grounds of Birr Castle, dates from the early 1820s.

CHAPTER TWO

BRIDGE TYPES
AND
MATERIALS

38

CARRICK-ON-SHANNON BRIDGE, COUNTY LEITRIM

During the 1840s, improvements to the Shannon Navigation required that many of the bridges spanning the river had to be rebuilt or replaced. Opening spans were normally provided for river traffic, but by the time the works had reached Carrick-on-Shannon in County Leitrim, money was running low and Thomas Rhodes designed a fixed bridge with sufficient headroom to accommodate the expected traffic. The spans increase slightly from 30ft to 35ft towards the centre of the river, and the parapet profile is only slightly curved, whilst the roadway is kept level over the central section of the bridge by small ramps at each end. The arch in the eastern abutment allows pedestrian access along the quayside.

ENNISCORTY BRIDGE, COUNTY WEXFORD

The town of Enniscorthy in County Wexford was founded on a hill overlooking the River Slaney at the limit of its tidal reach, the river being navigable from here to the sea at Wexford. A fine masonry bridge, built of local materials, spans the river at this point. The bridge dates from 1715, but was lowered and widened in 1836. Guarding the crossing on the west bank of the river stands a much repaired and altered Norman castle. The bridge has a curved approach span at the west end to accommodate the immediate junction of two main roads.

BECTIVE BRIDGE, COUNTY MEATH

Early bridges are often associated with nearby religious communities, and there are many records citing monks as the promoters of their building. Here, beside Bective Abbey in County Meath, the River Boyne is crossed by a solid stone bridge having eleven arches, varying in span from 10ft to 14ft. The profile of the arches are virtually circular, a form used from ancient times and repeated in thousands of smaller bridges throughout Ireland. The arch rings are formed of carefully laid dressed stones. By contrast, the spandrel walls are composed of courses of local rubble or fieldstone.

LONG BRIDGE, BELFAST

This 1917 watercolour by J.W.Carey was based on an old print depicting the Long Bridge at Belfast, which was built between 1682 and 1689. Seven of its twenty-one arches collapsed soon afterwards under the weight of Schomberg's artillery train. Repaired, it was not finally demolished until 1840 and, after some infilling on the east side of the River Lagan, was replaced by the present five-span Queen's Bridge in 1843. A stone bearing the name 'James Chad' was removed from the Long Bridge – presumably he was the master mason responsible for its construction.

SHANNONBRIDGE, COUNTY OFFALY

Following the surveys of the River Shannon by Thomas Rhodes in the 1830s, it was decided to retain the 18th century multi-span masonry arch bridge at Shannonbridge in County Offaly and to underpin the foundations. Excluding the navigation arch at the east end, the bridge has sixteen semicircular arches spanning between 6ft thick piers. There are extensive fortifications at the west end of the bridge, built in 1812 to withstand a perceived threat of invasion from the west by the forces of Napoleon.

MAGANEY BRIDGE, COUNTY CARLOW

As bridge spans increased, so did the loading on the foundations. One way of reducing the self-weight of a bridge structure was to use hollow spandrels, achieved by employing relieving arches spanning transversely across the tops of internal walls to form hollow compartments beneath the roadway. Alternatively, a cylindrical opening could be formed through the spandrel over each pier. However, more often than not, bridge designers, as here at Maganey over the River Barrow in County Carlow, blocked off the openings to form an attractive architectural feature.

BEALACLUGGA BRIDGE, COUNTY CLARE

During the 1820s there was extensive public road and bridge building in Ireland, much of it along the western seaboard. One of the government civil engineers, John Killaly, when faced in 1824 with bridging the Annagh River near Spanish Point in County Clare, elected to erect Bealaclugga Bridge, a single 'Gothic' arch of 34ft span springing between massive abutments and approach embankments. The embankment retaining walls are strengthened by masonry buttresses. The design style could be called 'castellated gothic' with considerable ornamentation, including a mixture of shields, rings and slits, and exhibits a flair for imagination and a desire to create something out of the ordinary.

GRAIGUENAMANAGH BRIDGE, COUNTY CARLOW

Designed with classic symmetry in the Palladian style by, it is believed, George Smith, a pupil of George Semple, this bridge spans the River Barrow at Graiguenamanagh in County Carlow. The spans increase from 19ft 4in. nearest the riverbank to 31ft 10in. in midstream. The voussoirs of the arch rings are formed from a light coloured slaty stone that contrasts with the darker material used in the spandrels. Over the piers on either side of the central arch there are architectural features known as pedimented aediculae and over the remaining piers circular recesses known as oculi.

ATHY HORSE BRIDGE, COUNTY KILDARE

The Barrow Line of the Grand Canal terminates at Athy in County Kildare where it joins the main river. In order to cross from the canal towpath to the left bank of the River Barrow, the horses drawing the barges used this narrow 'horse' bridge. This bridge, erected in 1791, was rebuilt in the 1880s.

KILLETER BRIDGE, COUNTY TYRONE

An example of a four-arch bridge built with a significant hump, which now constitutes a danger to modern traffic – a danger exacerbated by a T-junction located at the abutment. The manner in which the stone continues to rise across the two central arches to an apex over the central pier, suggests that the designer of Killeter Bridge in County Tyrone intended the whole structure to act as one large arch.

LUCAN BRIDGE, COUNTY DUBLIN

The largest single-span masonry arch bridge in Ireland crosses the River Liffey at Lucan in County Dublin. The architect and builder, George Knowles, created an aesthetically pleasing bridge with deep arch rings and spandrel walls of ashlar limestone. The iron balustraded parapets were cast in the foundry of the Royal Phoenix Ironworks in Dublin and are dated 1814. Although the largest in Ireland at 110ft, much larger spans have been built elsewhere. Although there is a weight restriction in operation, the bridge continues to tolerate heavy vehicles, a good indication of the inherent strength of well-constructed masonry arches.

WOLFENDEN'S BRIDGE, COUNTY ANTRIM/DOWN BORDER

By 1743, a bridge, then known as Lambeg Bridge, existed here, but Moll's map ignores this route. However, there is a strong local tradition that the wheel of King William's coach was broken whilst fording the River Lagan here in 1690. Wolfenden's Bridge on the County Antrim/Down border is a typical example of a field stone bridge. The arch shown on the left exhibits the effects of settlement of the fill and the remedial work undertaken to prevent further outward movement of the spandrel walls. This entailed placing iron bars with threaded ends through the bridge fill and securing them to flat plates bearing the vertical faces of the walls, thus restraining the walls from any tendency to bulge outwards.

COOKSTOWN PIPE BRIDGE, COUNTY WICKLOW

A more unusual type of bridge, its purpose being to carry the twin water mains of the Dublin Corporation's Vartry water supply across the Cookstown River near Enniskerry in County Wicklow. It is of iron latticework truss construction with a span of 45 ft. The stone portals through which the pipes pass are completed in a very ornate style. Water first flowed over the bridge in 1867, the ironwork being supplied and erected by Edington & Son of Glasgow.

RORY O'MORE BRIDGE, DUBLIN

Rory O'More Bridge is an example of a single span arch structure in cast-iron where the total dead weight has been reduced by using spandrels by openings (in this case, in the form of round-headed small arches). The outer arch rib carries the legend "Robert Daglish Junr St Helen's Foundry Lancashire 1858" cast into the metal. There are seven ribs at 5ft 6in. centres cross-braced internally in wrought-iron work. The span is 95ft between abutments of dressed granite. Built by John Killeen of Malahide, the bridge was opened in 1861 (as Victoria Bridge).

SEAN HEUSTON BRIDGE, DUBLIN

This single span cast-iron bridge was designed by George Papworth and opened in 1828. It spans 98ft across the River Liffey beside the main railway terminus of lines from Cork, Limerick, Waterford and Galway. The inner ribs have recently been replaced with steel, in order to accommodate the LUAS light rail transit system, but the ornamental outer spandrels been retained. Originally named Kings Bridge (to commemorate the visit to Dublin of George IV), the bridge was renamed Sean Heuston in honour of an Irish patriot.

SHANNON RAIL BRIDGE, COUNTY WESTMEATH

The River Shannon at Athlone in County Westmeath presented a formidable barrier to the railway builders in laying their line westward to Galway. The difficulty in forming the 1 diameter foundation piers in the soft riverbed was overcome by the use of compressed air, a very early use of this technique. The designer of the Shannon Rail Bridge was G W Hemans and the contractor Fox Henderson & Co. Opened in 1851, the bridge has a twin-leaf cable-stayed central swing section (now welded shut) approached from either side by wrought-iron bowstring girders, 20ft 4in. maximum depth and spanning 176ft.

Bridge Types *and* Materials

The outermost supports of a bridge are known as the abutments. These may have a vertical face or follow the slope of the ground. Single span bridges have no other supports, whilst additional intermediate supports in the form of piers or columns are a feature of bridges having more than one span. The term span usually denotes the distance between the supports of a bridge; it is usually measured as the clear distance between the face of one pier and the next, but is sometimes measured from the centre of one pier to the centre of the next. Spans may vary in multi-span bridges.

A bridge may be provided to carry road, rail or pedestrian traffic, or sometimes services, over or under some obstruction to free passage. Applying European Commission directives for heavy goods vehicle loading, a bridge is normally defined as one having a span of greater than two metres.

RATHDRUM VIADUCT,
COUNTY WICKOW

Small structures may be referred to as culverts, although in Grand Jury presentments, culverts are often called pipes, some being arched, others being of square section. A few examples of a series of culverts being provided in place of a bridge have been noted. This form of construction is useful when the bed of a stream is close to the road level, the hump associated with an arch being avoided. However, culverts are less suitable in rivers that flood,

STRAMATT BRIDGE, COUNTY CAVAN

An example of an early multi-span stone arch bridge spanning the Boyne Blackwater where it exits from Lough Ramor to the south of Virginia in County Cavan. The nine-arch Stramatt Bridge is shown on Moll's map of 1719, but the construction of a new mail coach road further to the south resulted in it being relegated to serve what is now a minor road.

STONE CULVERT BRIDGE, COUNTY FERMANAGH

An example of a multiple box culvert bridge constructed in stone. There are six parallel box sections laid side by side to provide the necessary flow capacity, each of 16in. width. In this example, the stream crosses the line of the road at a marked angle, or skew, and it is possible that this form of structure was found to be easier to plan and build than a skew bridge. The thin layer of filling between the flat lintels and the level road surface is readily apparent. The structure is near Belleek in County Fermanagh, close to the border with County Donegal.

PORT BRIDGE,
COUNTY DONEGAL

The replacement for the Port Bridge crossing the River Swilly at Letterkenny in County Donegal was completed using five parallel Armco culverts of the more usual arch section. The sides have been completed to complement the slopes of the road approach embankments. Similar examples have recently been constructed in other parts of the country.

as they constitute more of an obstruction to flow. A reinforced concrete box culvert is a form of construction where the roof, walls and floor are all of a similar thickness, the applied loads being distributed throughout the structure. Spans may be appreciably over two metres. The recent introduction of Armco culverts, an American design in corrugated steel with an arched roof and dished floor, and often of appreciable span, has provided an economical form of bridge construction for small to intermediate spans.

High multi-span bridges are frequently referred to as viaducts, whilst bridges conveying water are known as aqueducts, usually being of multi-arch construction. Small accommodation bridges may be provided for use by farm animals (and sometimes for wild life

CONN O'NEILL'S BRIDGE,
BELFAST

Regarded by the DoE for NI as probably the oldest bridge in Ulster, this is a single arch stone structure in the packhorse style. It crosses the River Connswater in Belfast and is sometimes referred to as Conn O'Neill's Bridge. It is believed that the bridge lies on the route of the track-way to the O'Neill's stronghold, which would date the bridge to around 1600.

such as badgers) whilst so-called pipe bridges are designed to carry services. Bridges have also featured in the landscaping of some large country houses, either as decorative, yet functional, structures spanning a river or lake, as part of the imposing entrances to the estates, or simply as folly bridges.

Four types of force act on a bridge, either singly, or in combination. Tension, which stretches or pulls the construction material apart, is the opposite of compression, which squeezes or pushes it together. Shear is a sliding force, whilst torsion is a twisting force. The

structural engineer is now able to calculate accurately the forces acting on and in a structure, but much was done in the past by rule-of-thumb. Bridges, where there was any uncertainty concerning the estimated forces, were usually test loaded on completion.

A bridge must resist the forces or stresses to which it is subjected, both during the construction sequence and after completion. Bridges need to be designed to carry their own weight, the dead load and to carry traffic, the live load, as well as having to resist natural and

BENNET'S BRIDGE, COUNTY KILKENNY

Bennet's Bridge in County Kilkenny illustrates the problems faced by modern traffic in negotiating hump-backed bridges. There are six semi-circular arches of varying span, which increase in span and rise towards the centre of the river. Built in the 1760s, the bridge spans the River Nore and, despite the problems caused by its profile, continues to carry modern traffic on this important route.

environmental forces. Over the life of the bridge, care needs to be taken not to increase the dead load by adding extra weight, for example by laying a deeper roadway. For example, work inspired by the Irish Post Office on mail coach routes often involved the removal of the tops of hills and the filling of hollows – a process that left some bridges with a deeper layer of fill over the arch. Later in the 19th century, some bridges were built with thin arches on high abutments in order to reduce the gradient of the approaches, such approaches often having high retaining walls, some of which proving troublesome over time. On the other hand, new materials may be used to reduce the dead weight.

BORRIS VIADUCT, COUNTY CARLOW

Rail traffic could not cope with steep gradients and, as a result, viaducts were built to carry railways across valleys. Borris viaduct in County Carlow, with its sixteen spans, each of 35ft, is typical of the construction in stone of such viaducts, in this instance using limestone. The viaduct was built in 1862 on the Bagenalstown to Wexford Railway. The line did not prove to be a great success, passenger services being suspended in 1931 and the line closing completely in 1963, leaving the viaduct, like a number in Ireland, abandoned. The engineer for the 470ft long structure was William le Fanu and the contractor John Bagnall.

LEINSTER AQUEDUCT,
COUNTY KILDARE

The Leinster aqueduct, carrying the Grand Canal over the River Liffey to the west of Sallins in County Kildare, was designed by Richard Evans, construction commencing in 1780. The sides and bottom of the canal are lined with 'puddled' clay to form an effective impervious seal against egress of water from the navigation. The five-arch aqueduct is constructed in ashlar limestone masonry.

Over the years, the live loads to be carried have increased dramatically with the heavier commercial vehicles now in use. Fortunately, in many cases, this extra load has been accommodated on early stone bridges due to the inherent strength of masonry arch construction. It has also been suggested that increasing the number of vehicle axles reduces the impact of the heavier loads on a bridge structure, but recent research suggests that this may represent an over-simplification of the effect of increasing traffic loadings on the life of a structure. Modern fast moving vehicles may sharply impact onto the bridge deck and their

passage may also cause vibration of the structure - for some years, a hinged 'relieving slab' was added to the approach of some concrete bridges to reduce the effect of impact, but these are now regarded as not having been satisfactory and are no longer used. The most important natural load to be carried is the wind as, fortunately, bridges in Ireland do not have to withstand the effects of mining subsidence or earthquakes. However, the weight of floodwater, riverbed erosion, both increased by the presence of piers within a river channel, and frost, can all cause damage.

BARROW RAIL BRIDGE, COUNTY WATERFORD

The long rail bridge spanning the River Barrow to the east of Waterford exemplifies the modified Pratt trusses used in a number of such bridges. It was completed in 1906 as part of a new direct line between Waterford and Rosslare Harbour (now Rosslare Europort) in County Wexford, undertaken as a joint promotion by English and Irish railway companies to improve access to cross-channel passenger services. There are thirteen fixed spans and one swivel span in the 2132ft long structure, probably the longest such structure over water in Ireland. The designer was Sir Benjamin Baker and the steelwork was supplied and erected by Sir William Arrol of Glasgow, both having previously been involved with the building of the Forth Rail Bridge in Scotland.

GOVERNOR'S BRIDGE, BELFAST

Governor's Bridge has the lowest clearance of any of Belfast's River Lagan bridges. This presented a problem when a cycleway was added in 2001 on the left bank of the river. The base of the cycleway had to be taken down below water-level and pumps installed to prevent its flooding.

UPPER DUNMURRY LANE BRIDGE, BELFAST

The single span, three-centred, arch bridge on Upper Dunmurry Lane on the outskirts of Belfast was built of sandstone blocks by Thomas Jackson Woodhouse (County Surveyor for Antrim) for the Ulster Railway in 1839. Whilst considered quite adequate when built, it is now too low for some modern traffic. Fortunately, high-sided vehicles may use the adjacent level crossing. The low arch has been highlighted by painting in contrasting yellow and black 'rays' to draw the attention of approaching drivers to the hazard.

The various types of bridge structures differ in the way each carries the loads. The simplest, the beam bridge, is horizontally self-supporting and exerts a downward force on its piers. A plank of timber, or a stone slab, laid across a stream forms a beam and is considered to be simply supported. Recent excavations at Clonmacnoise on the River Shannon in County Offaly of a bridge dated to 804 A.D. have suggested that it consisted of two parallel rows of vertical timbers spaced every 18ft and cross-braced in pairs, with a timber deck of planks laid

on longitudinal bearers, similar to timber bridges erected by the Roman legions.

Although a few early stone bridges had flat stone lintels, most took the form of a series of arches. Once erected, arch bridges are by their nature very stable. The arch force is carried outward from the centre to the ends, where the abutments are required to exert a compressive force to keep the arch from spreading. Occasionally the bases of the abutments are tied together below water/ground level to guard against the possibility of spreading. The

DRUMSNA BRIDGE, COUNTY ROSCOMMON

This late 17th century bridge at Drumsna over the River Shannon in County Roscommon serves to illustrate the variety of maintenance work to which such a bridge may be subjected, although its original 16ft width and the pedestrian refuges have been retained. There was a need to protect the piers with concrete skirts to prevent their being undermined by river scour. The spandrel walls of the bridge had obviously shown signs of trying to splay outwards, thus the walls have been tied together by rods passing from side to side and bearing on so-called patress plates, which are clearly visible in the photograph. The soffit of the arch nearest to the camera has been strengthened by spraying with concrete. Work has also been undertaken on the parapet, unfortunately in brick, not a particularly suitable material to use for the repair of such a stone structure of undoubted heritage value.

FERMOY BRIDGE, COUNTY CORK

Contrasting with Stramatt Bridge on page 40, Fermoy Bridge is representative of later structures built with well dressed stone blocks or ashlar masonry. Rounded cutwaters in dressed stone seem to be a feature of such 19th century bridges. It was designed by A.O.Lyons and built by Joshua Hargreave in 1865. The seven segmental arches over the Munster Blackwater have spans varying between 38ft and 48ft 4in. This stone bridge, being of quite late construction, was built to a generous width of 41ft to serve the main road from Dublin to Cork.

THIN ARCH STONE STRUCTURE, BELFAST/DUBLIN RAIL LINE

Close-up of a thin arch stone structure on the Belfast to Dublin railway line. Note the use of long voussoir stones to form the arch ring.

construction of bridges crossing an obstacle at an angle, or skew, was not fully understood until towards the end of the 18th century, thus many bridges were designed to cross at right angles and were approached by sharp bends in the roadway.

A load applied to a beam causes it to deflect downwards and to bend, the magnitude of which effect is quantified as the bending moment to be resisted. Multi-span simply supported bridges may be encountered, there being a clear joint in the deck at each support. A continuous beam, by contrast, extends structurally over a number of supports provided

along its length. Deep beams in metal are sometimes referred to as girders, the web (the metal between the upper and lower flanges) being either open latticed work or solid plate.

A cantilever is a beam extending from a bridge pier to a free end, which may be propped by a second pier, or two arms may extend from opposite sides to meet at the centre. On one of the first major structures in Ireland in this form, Butt Bridge in Dublin, each cellular cantilevered beam is counterbalanced by an approach span of solid construction, the effect of the propping at the centre being ignored in the design calculations. Sometimes the arms carry

CORRATAVEY BRIDGE, COUNTY ANTRIM

One of the first contracts undertaken in sections by the Commissioners of Public Works was the reconstruction of the Antrim Coast road to a design by William Bald. The largest bridge in the first section across Cushleake Mountain is Corratavey, 136ft long and built with high abutments. Corratavey has 'WILLIAM BALD ENGINEER' inscribed on the parapet. The tall arch proportions (47ft by 18ft) are replicated on Bald's thumbnail sketch for Glendun viaduct, completed later, probably by Sir Charles Lanyon.

a simply supported drop-in centre section. The arms support the mid-section by the force of tension whilst the piers absorb the downward force. In some modern bridges, cantilevers are built out to either side of a pier resulting in a balanced load distribution on the pier.

An alternative to beams and cantilevers is the truss. A truss is made up of many small-section structural members, arranged in such a manner that the tension and compressive forces within the members balance each other out across the truss (see chapter on metal bridges). Trusses normally exhibit a rectangular form in elevation, the arrangement of

PETTIGO STATION BRIDGE, COUNTY DONEGAL

This now redundant structure near Pettigo station in County Donegal was built in 1865 to carry the Bundoran branch line railway. The river is crossed at a marked skew and the masons have countered this by using spiral coursing in the arch barrel. Note also how the horizontal courses in the face of the bridge have been married to the stones of the arch ring by locally using blocks of a height equal to about half of those used in the remainder.

HILLSBOROUGH AQUEDUCT, NR COUNTY DOWN

Reference is made elsewhere to Fairbairn's large box-girder bridges. This example at Hillsborough in County Down is an example on a much smaller scale. Here, the box girder is used to convey a surface stream over a cutting on the Banbridge, Lisburn and Belfast Railway of 1861, the line of the railway having been laid across that of the surface drainage. Although this line has been closed for almost fifty years, the box continues to serve its original purpose – the only alternative would be to allow the stream to flow into and along the former track-bed. It is surprising that such structures are found infrequently, given that any quality local metal working enterprise could have supplied and erected them.

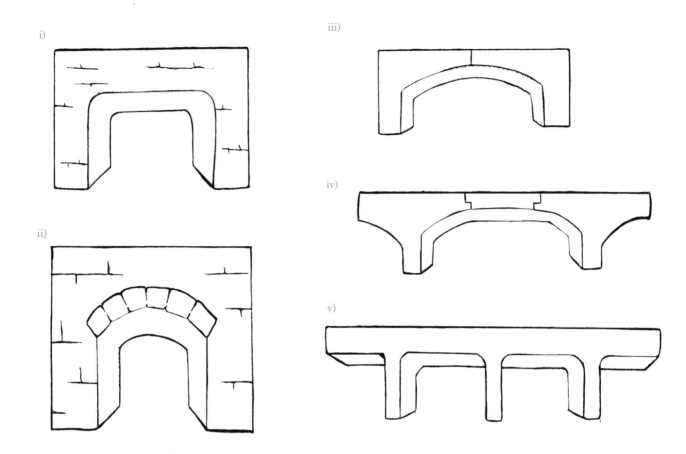

TYPES OF BRIDGE STRUCTURE
i) Simply supported beam
ii) Arch
iii) Double cantilever
iv) Cantilevers with drop-in central section
v) Beam continuous over two spans, with end cantilevers

members determining the type. When the top member is curved, such trusses are referred to as bowstring. Truss spans may be simple or continuous. The deck carrying traffic may be supported from the bottom of a truss or girder (known as the through type) or across the top of the truss or girder. Although sometimes omitted on canal aqueducts on the side opposite to a towpath, and on railway viaducts, most bridge decks are provided with side parapets. Some of the early narrow stone bridges incorporate recessed refuges over the piers in which a pedestrian could seek protection from other traffic.

Bridge supports need a firm foundation to withstand the ravages of time. Wherever possible, a foundation is carried down to firm ground, in some cases to solid rock. In the case of certain of the later bridges, substantial foundations were provided by the sinking of large tubes, or caissons, through the soft layers to the underlying firmer ground. These caissons had to be de-watered by pumping or the use of compressed air before construction could

BOYNE VIADUCT, COUNTY LOUTH

The last obstacle to railway communication between Dublin and Belfast was the crossing of the River Boyne near Drogheda, where headroom of 90ft had to be provided to meet Admiralty requirements. Wrought-iron latticed trusses were selected for the three spans of the bridge (141ft, 267ft, and 141ft), with semicircular stone arch approach viaducts to either side. The detailed drawings were prepared by James Barton, although the design concept has been credited to Sir John Macneill. Constructed between 1851 and 1855, it represented an early example of the large-scale use of wrought-iron trusses. As a consequence, the structure was thoroughly test-loaded on completion as illustrated in the lower picture.

The strength of the original Boyne Viaduct was called into question as early as 1860, and again in 1900, when a 20 mph speed restriction was imposed. In 1930, it was found that considerable rusting of the wrought-iron had occurred and the structure was replaced in steel. The curved top member of the truss was introduced to provide for a more aesthetically pleasing structure. The original superstructure was replaced without any interruption to rail traffic. This was achieved by building the new structure within the original trusses and gradually transferring the load.

LAYTOWN VIADUCT, COUNTY MEATH

Twin-track rail viaduct spanning the River Nanny at Laytown in County Meath on the mainline between Dublin and Belfast. The original latticed girder bridge of 1844, was replaced in 1896. It consisted of three 60ft spans of 6ft deep double latticed steel girders with 30ft plate girder side spans supported on 5ft 6in. diameter cast-iron cylindrical columns. These girders were, in turn, renewed in 1996 as part of the upgrading of the Dublin-Belfast route.

commence. The use of driven timbers under a raft foundation to provide extra support is an early invention, the Romans having been known to employ such a technique. Timber piles from the 17th century recovered from Shaw's Bridge in Belfast, were found to have metal strengtheners at both top and point. Piles are now made of reinforced concrete, or sometimes, although there may be a problem with rusting, of steel.

Timber or stone was used in the construction of early bridges. With the advent of widespread industrialisation, brick, iron, steel and concrete all came into use, whilst some modern bridges have employed the lighter metal aluminium. Bridges of composite construction use different materials that act together structurally, the most obvious example being reinforced concrete. Having become so widely employed, it can be regarded as a construction material in its own right. There are some instances of stone and brick structures with a mass concrete core, or 'hearting', and stone bridges with brick arches. One of the last uses in Ireland of this technique was probably for the bridges built by Robert McAlpine in

CRAIGAVON BRIDGE, COUNTY DERRY

Access to the city of Derry across the River Foyle was by ferry until 1791 when a timber bridge was erected. In 1863, a twin-deck (road over rail) iron bridge was completed, which in turn was replaced by Derry CBC in 1933 by the present Craigavon Bridge. This was designed by Mott Hay & Anderson, Dorman Long & Co. supplying the structural steel. There are five double-deck 130ft spans comprised of Pratt trusses, and seventeen single-deck approach spans, totalling in all some 1260ft in length. The cylindrical piers are founded 69ft below high water level. In 1968, the lower dual-gauge rail-deck was converted for road use and the decks strengthened in 2000.

BALLINA BRIDGE, COUNTY MAYO

One of two bridges spanning the River Moy in Ballina in County Mayo, the bridge illustrated having been completed using a mixture of brick and stone in a manner similar to some railway structures. On these, the faces were in stone, whilst brick was used in the arch barrels. At Ballina by contrast, brick has been used to form the three-centred arch rings as may be seen in the photograph.

1909 on the Strabane to Letterkenny railway in County Donegal. These had stone faces and abutments and a mass concrete arch. Some structures use a variety of materials, the bridge over the Ballindrait River on the same railway providing a good example. This had steel trusses carried by concrete cradles supported on stone piers, with massive concrete abutments taken down the face of the riverbank to below the bed of the river.

The first suspension bridge recorded in Britain was that erected over the River Tees in 1741 (collapsed 1802). The deck was laid on the main support cables that passed over towers to anchorages at either end. The cables (and thus the deck) followed a curved or catenary profile over the length of the bridge – a design still to be seen at Carrick-a-Rede in County

CURRAGHANOE BRIDGE, COUNTY CAVAN

Curraghanoe Bridge, near Ballyhaise in County Cavan, is an example of Mouchel's standard beam and slab bridge deck completed in Hennebique concrete. Built by J & R Thompson in 1909-10, the narrow 10 ft wide structure, with three 32 ft spans, almost certainly replaced a timber deck. It is now in poor condition and carries a two-tonne weight restriction and a 2.9 m height restriction.

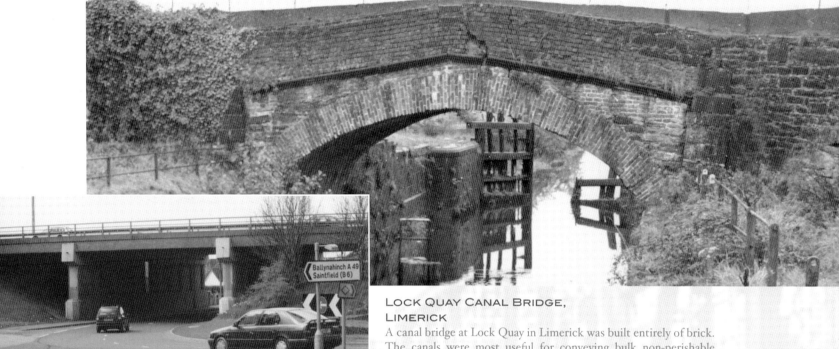

LOCK QUAY CANAL BRIDGE, LIMERICK

A canal bridge at Lock Quay in Limerick was built entirely of brick. The canals were most useful for conveying bulk non-perishable goods, brick being a good example. The canals were thus instrumental in making brick available as a building material to parts of Ireland where they had not been used previously.

EARLY MOTORWAY BRIDGE, COUNTY ANTRIM

A motorway interchange bridge, built in 1963 on the first section of the M1 in Northern Island near Lisburn in County Antrim. The massive proportions of these early motorway structures may be readily appreciated from the illustration.

Antrim. The true suspension bridge, with a level deck hung off the cables by suspenders, appears to have originated in Asia. (Such bridges with chain cables are recorded in China from the second or third century). It is sometimes claimed that General Wellesley (afterwards the Duke of Wellington) introduced this type of bridge from India during the Peninsular War and examples have certainly been recorded in Britain from about 1810. A variation, which has recently returned to popularity, is the cable-stayed bridge, in which the deck is supported

i)
ii)

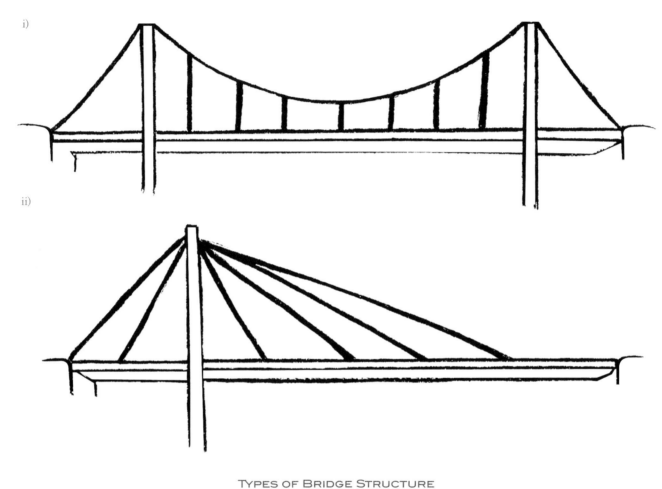

TYPES OF BRIDGE STRUCTURE
i) Suspension
ii) Cable-stayed

directly off the towers by a series of radiating or parallel cables. Suspension cables are in tension, the pull being withstood by the anchorage and the towers themselves being in compression. In some steel or concrete arch bridges, the deck may be suspended in whole or in part from the top member.

Movable bridges form a distinct group. They are almost always built over water and open to allow the passage of vessels. They permit the construction of lower approach embankments than would be needed for a fixed span bridge, but obviously subject the traffic passing over the bridge to periodic delay. A swing bridge may pivot about a central pier, or be built as two identical halves pivoting about the abutments. In a bascule type bridge, the deck is hinged

JERRETTS PASS BRIDGE, COUNTY DOWN
This bridge over the Newry Canal at Jerretts Pass in County Down, with its rather unusual parapet profile rising to a point and with end roundels, has been attributed to the canal engineer John Brownrigg (ca1808).

LIFFEY (HA'PENNY) BRIDGE, DUBLIN
End detail of the Liffey Bridge in Dublin illustrating how the thrust of an arch bridge may be resisted more efficiently by the use of a skew-back.

STRAFFAN SUSPENSION BRIDGE, COUNTY KILDARE

This small suspension bridge at Straffan House (now a golf club) in County Kildare employs a single cable, whereas earlier bridges used a bundled wire cable. The Straffan bridge was manufactured and erected in 1849 by the Dublin firm of Courtney and Stephens. Bridges of this type, especially when the handrail provides little stiffening as here, are very flexible and move underfoot - a motion that many may find disturbing. To counteract this, the deck was stiffened with a concrete slab at a more recent date

COURTNEY & STEPHENS
DUBLIN   1849

about one end and is normally raised and lowered with the aid of a counterweighted mechanism. Drawbridges are similar and are opened by a rope, cable or chain from above. In a lift bridge, sometimes called a guillotine bridge, the central horizontal section is raised and lowered vertically.

With increasing traffic flows, bridges have frequently had to be widened, in many cases in order to separate vehicular from pedestrian traffic. There are numbers of examples of stone arch bridges widened on one side only, sometimes more than once. This can result in the two

BOWSTRING ARCH BRIDGE,
COUNTY KERRY
Detail of the central support of the reinforced concrete bowstring arch bridge near Kenmare in County Kerry, which is founded on a rock outcrop. An earlier suspension bridge from the 1840s used this support and the existing stonework in the pier and abutment foundations probably dates from this period.

faces of the bridge being completed with different detailing. Increasingly, however, materials like cast-iron and concrete were used to cantilever off the existing structure on both sides to provide the extra width, the results not always being the most aesthetically pleasing. Examples of major bridges widened in this way include Grattan Bridge in Dublin (1875) and the Queen's Bridge in Belfast (1886). Increasing loads, deepening of river

DALY'S BRIDGE, CORK

Daly's Bridge in Cork is a fine example of a suspension bridge, unusual in the lightness and complexity of its latticed towers, which support pairs of 1.5 in. diameter cables that are only required to carry a 4ft 6in. wide footpath with low loading. Built by David Rowell, Engineers, of London in 1927, the bridge was a gift to Cork Corporation from James Daly. It crosses the River Lee at Sunday's Well in the city with a span approaching 150 ft; the towers are 12ft 6in. high. A bridge of almost identical design built near Sion Mills in County Tyrone in 1930 was overturned in a flood when the mass-concrete tower bases sheared under the weight of water.

GRATTAN BRIDGE, DUBLIN

When Essex (later renamed Grattan) Bridge in Dublin was rebuilt in 1875, the designer, Bindon Stoney, elected to provide for pedestrian traffic by supporting footpaths either side on cantilevered wrought-iron frames bolted through to the masonry. Stoney also used wrought-iron for the parapets, which are substantial double-latticed girders with cast-iron ornamentation. A similar arrangement was used for the Queen's Bridge in Belfast.

SHERIFF STREET BRIDGE, DUBLIN

An example of an opening bridge of the drawbridge type, the weight of the deck being balanced by the high-level beam. This bridge carries Sheriff Street over the Royal Canal at Spencer Dock in Dublin and was installed in the 1930s. This view highlights the rather utilitarian nature of such bridges.

channels to improve land drainage, and other factors, have resulted in some bridge foundations having to be underpinned, that is carried down to a deeper level.

The reluctance of the early designers to build on the skew has left a legacy of old bridges built at right angles to the intervening obstacle and thus approached by sharp bends. Whilst this was acceptable when traffic speeds were low, the arrangement is unsafe when modern traffic speeds and vehicle lengths are taken into account. Also,

bridges built in the horse and cart era may not now have sufficient height clearance to accommodate double-decker buses and other high-sided vehicles. This is a particular problem with railway under-bridges, as to increase the clearance would require raising the level of the track over a considerable distance, with a likely knock-on effect on adjacent bridges. Humped back bridges were often built over canals to provide the necessary clearance for boats and now constitute a potential hazard for vehicular traffic.❖

LUCAN BRIDGE BALLUSTRADES,
COUNTY DUBLIN
Detail of the cast-iron ballustrading on Lucan Bridge over the River Liffey near Dublin.
The foundry mark reads 'PHOENIX IRON-WORKS DUBLIN 1814'.

LISPOLE VIADUCT,
COUNTY KERRY

Completed in 1891, the 3ft narrow-gauge railway from Tralee to Dingle traversed some of the wildest hill country in Ireland. The viaduct near the village of Lispole consists of two 50ft steel lattice girders approached each side by 30ft span stone arches. Fifty years after the last train passed by, the work of the contractor Robert Worthington still stands boldly defying the elements.

CHAPTER THREE

STONE BRIDGES

Stone Bridges

Surviving road bridges built in Ireland prior to the middle of the nineteenth century are generally of stone. Such bridges are often referred to as masonry bridges, implying that the skill of a stonemason was employed by the promoters of the bridge. A cursory examination of a stone bridge will often indicate the level of skill involved, not only by the mason but, in more recent times, by the architect or engineer. Stone bridges were

frequently built to replace earlier timber structures that had become unstable, or had been carried away by floodwaters, or erected as a substitute for a ford.

Although a tradition of using stone for building could be said to date from pre-Christian times (Newgrange and Gallurus Oratory being examples), it was not until the coming of the Cistercians (1148) and the Normans (1169) that the erection of stone arch structures of any significance began to be considered. The voissoir arch, an essential element of any stone arch bridge, is believed to have originated independently in various parts of the ancient world. It is reasonable to suggest that a local style of arch bridge design may well have been evolving in Ireland prior to the coming of the Normans.

SCARAWALSH BRIDGE,
COUNTY WEXFORD

The shape of the arch profile gives some indication of the age of a stone bridge, but must be taken in conjunction with many other factors. Semicircular arches were generally introduced into Ireland in the 12th century, or perhaps somewhat earlier. Pointed segmental arch construction followed later. The three-centred arch is said to have originated in the 16th century. From it, the false ellipse profile was developed that later became the standard for canal and railway over-bridges where headroom was a critical factor. Flat segmental arches became common after 1750 when the balancing of the horizontal thrusting forces was better understood.

NEWTOWN TRIM BRIDGE, COUNTY MEATH

This bridge over the River Boyne at Newtown Trim in County Meath was reputedly sponsored by William Sherwood, Bishop of Meath, and erected between 1460 and 1475. The abutments and piers are founded on rock and this fact has probably contributed to the ability of the structure to withstand the many floods within the river over the years. The presence of rock also prevented scouring from under the piers that, on numerous occasions, has led to the collapse of other early bridges. The upstream cutwaters are formed of massive masonry of triangular cross-section capped by a triangular prism of masonry, an innovative design for the period.

ABBEYTOWN BRIDGE, COUNTY SLIGO

This five-span stone arch bridge over the Boyle Water in County Sligo leads to the former Cistercian Monastery in Boyle. According to O'Keeffe (1991), the most likely period for its construction is between 1190 and 1220 and it seems never to have been widened or rebuilt. The massive triangular cutwaters on the upstream face extend up to road level and are capped with flat stone slabs. All but one of the arch rings have intrados formed of circular arcs, the most easterly one being pointed segmental. The material of construction is mainly locally occurring sandstone with some limestone. Abbeytown Bridge marks the transition between the traditional Irish and Anglo-Norman forms of construction.

The Normans were masters of the art of building in stone and built castles at or near fords and crossing points along the major rivers, such as at Athlone in County Westmeath and at Limerick across the river Shannon, as bridgeheads for further expansion. By controlling navigation and crossing points, they were able to regulate communications. The great stone castle building period in Ireland extended from about 1180 to around 1310, thus there was a continuous demand for masons and carpenters. In many cases, towns grew up around the castles and markets developed, leading to the need for safer river crossings in the form of more substantial stone bridges. Notable stone bridges constructed during the 14th century include that over the River Liffey at Kilcullen in County Kildare (1319) and at Leighlinbridge over the River Barrow in County Carlow (1320)(see p.14).

The *Masonry Arch Bridge*

'**S**uppose for instance, we are present at the building of a bridge : the bricklayers or masons have had their centering erected for them, and that centering was put together by a carpenter, who had the line of its curve traced for him by the architect : the masons are dexterously handling and fitting their bricks, or, by the help of machinery, carefully adjusting stones, which are numbered for their places. There is probably in their quickness of eye and readiness of hand something admirable : but this is not what I ask the reader to admire : not the carpentering, nor the bricklaying, nor anything that he can presently see and understand, but the choice of the curve, and the shaping of the numbered stones, and the appointment of that number; there were many things to be known and thought upon before there were decided. The man who chose the curve and numbered the stones, had to know the times and tides of the river, and the strength of its floods, and the height and flow of them, and the soil of the banks, and the endurance of it, and the weight of the stones he had to build with, and the kind of traffic that day by day would be carried on over his bridge – all this especially, and all the great general laws of force and weight, and their working; and in the choice of the curve and numbering of stones are expressed not only his knowledge of these, but such ingenuity and firmness as he had, in applying special means to overcome the special difficulties about his bridge. There is no saying how much wit, how much depth of thought, how much fancy, presence of mind, courage, and fixed resolution there may have gone to the placing of a single stone of it. '*

John Ruskin,
The Stones of Venice, 1853

DRUMCONDRA BRIDGE, DUBLIN

The main road north from Dublin spans the River Tolka at Drumcondra in Dublin. People crossing the bridge may pause to admire the pierced balustrades, but rarely, if ever, look further to appreciate the work of the master mason responsible for the fine cut-stone arch rings. Similar balustrading may be seen on other bridges, for example Ballsbridge in Dublin and St Patrick's in Cork.

LONGWOOD, COUNTY MEATH

Road meets rail and canal near Longwood in County Meath. The rail line from Dublin runs parallel to the Royal Canal for much of the way to Mullingar. The railway bridge in the foreground, with its fine ashlar masonry, was erected in 1849 and matches the stone work of the earlier canal aqueduct completed in 1804.

KEY STONE

COPING

PARAPET

STRING COURSE

SPANDREL

ARCH RING OF
VOUSSOIRS

EXTRADOS

INTRADOS

BARREL

SKEWBACK

SPRINGING

THE ELEMENTS OF A MASONRY ARCH

Carpentry and stonemasonry were the main trades involved in the construction of bridges in Ireland up until the middle of the 16th century. Skilled or journeyman masons travelled from job to job, carrying their tools with them. Many would have come to Ireland from across the Irish Sea or possibly from as far away as continental Europe. Their trade was well established and was to make a vital contribution to the development of trade routes in Ireland and elsewhere. During the 16th century, numbers of substantial stone bridges were erected, for example across the Boyne at Kilcarn near Navan in County Meath and in the larger towns of Ballinasloe, Carlow and Enniscorthy.

The 1634 Act was of great importance, not only for bridges, but because it was the origin of the establishment of the Grand Juries and the so-called 'presentment' system for financing. This system introduced the concept of seeking approval for the construction of public and private works. A paucity of surviving records in Ireland has prevented any real insight into bridge construction during the period up to the middle of the 17th century. There are, of course, exceptions, notably the descriptions of major bridges that played central roles in various military campaigns, such as the Old Long Bridge across the Lagan in Belfast, the bridges across the Shannon at Limerick and Athlone and the bridge across the Boyne at Slane in County Meath. Between 1670 and 1684, four new stone bridges were erected across the River Liffey in Dublin, but all have since been rebuilt.

RIVERSTOWN BRIDGE, COUNTY OFFALY/TIPPERARY BORDER

A small 18th century multi-arch masonry road bridge spanning the Little Brosna River at Riverstown on the County Offaly/Tipperary border a few miles southwest of Birr. The cutwaters have been extended up to parapet level to provide pedestrian refuges, a feature of many early bridges. These are as much needed today as in former years, as the bridge continues to withstand the onslaught of modern traffic on the N52 trunk road.

SIR THOMAS'S BRIDGE, COUNTY TIPPERARY

Sponsored by Sir Thomas Osborne, who died in 1713, this late 17th century stone bridge to the east of Clonmel in County Tipperary has been altered and repaired on a number of occasions during its long life. In the 1750s, to assist the passage of vessels using the Suir Navigation, a single arch of 55ft span with a rise of 15ft was created within the structure. As with many bridges of either local or regional strategic importance, the bridge suffered damage in 1922 during the Civil War. The inherent strength of masonry arch bridges limited the damage and the bridge should survive for many more years to come.

FLORENCE COURT ESTATE BRIDGE, COUNTY FERMANAGH

This estate bridge at Florence Court in County Fermanagh carried a minor road over what was the private carriage ride to the deer park. It is unusual in that the stonework for the single span and the long approach ramps are all apparently laid 'dry', that is without the use of mortar. What appear to be stone voissoirs are no more than a thin surface feature, the arch barrel being of dry-laid fieldstone. Now abandoned, vegetation had taken root and will in time, if left unchecked, destroy this remarkable structure.

INISCARRA BRIDGE, COUNTY CORK

Spanning the River Lee to the west of the Gunpowder Mills at Ballincollig in County Cork, Iniscarra Bridge probably dates from around 1700, but was rebuilt by Charles Wilks, superintendent of the mills, in 1805. The twelve semicircular arches, of which five are fully visible in the photograph, increase gently in height towards the centre of the bridge. The rough voissoirs are of sandstone and limestone, both of which occur locally. To the south-southeast, a further six small semicircular arches with paved stone beds provide flood relief.

The vast majority of pre-1750 stone bridges in Ireland are likely to have been planned and built by stonemasons. However from around 1750 onwards, most large bridges were designed, and their construction supervised by engineers, and occasionally by architects. From then, until the end of the century and into the 19th century, there is evidence of a Palladian

influence in the design of a number of major road bridges, particularly in the more affluent areas of the south east of the country and in Dublin. The four-volume work of the 16th century architect, Andrea Palladio, was translated into English in 1738 by Isaac Ware. Ware published his Complete Body of Architecture in 1755 and one of his designs was later used by Thomas Ivory for the Classical Bridge in the demesne of Carton House in County Kildare. On occasions, the entrances to such stately homes have incorporated architectural follies in the form of bridge structures, the late Victorian six-arch castellated bridge forming the entrance to Ashford Castle near Cong in County Mayo being a fine example.

TRIM BRIDGE,
COUNTY MEATH

Probably the oldest unaltered bridge in existence today in Ireland, the bridge at Trim over the River Boyne is believed to date from 1393. It is founded on rock, has four pointed segmental masonry arches of 16ft span and piers of 8ft thickness. The arch rings are formed of roughly trimmed rectangular stones of varying thickness, the spandrel masonry being of roughly coursed random rubble. The river was lowered by 4ft during the 1970s and the base of each pier surrounded with a reinforced concrete skirt to counter the scouring action of floodwaters.

There are records of a wooden bridge
spanning the River Shannon at Killaloe in
County Clare in Norman times, but the bridge had
disappeared by the 14th century and the crossing probably
reverted to a ford. The present bridge dates from the 17th century
and had originally nineteen arches. The west end was altered about 1780
to accommodate the Limerick-Killaloe Navigation and all but five of the
remaining arches, each of 20ft span, were replaced in 1843 with eight
segmental arches of 40ft span. This considerably improved the flow in
the river. A fixed metal girder span was added in 1929 to provide
increased headroom for river traffic.

The word 'design' is of French origin and usually means 'to draw, to form a plan, or to
contrive'. In the second half of the 18th century, bridge designers drew heavily on French
engineering practice. The Parisian architect and bridge engineer, Jean-Rodolphe Perronet
(1708-96), was the first to discover that the horizontal thrust of the arches was carried
through the arch spans and that the piers carry only the vertical load and the difference
between the thrusts of the adjacent arch spans. By keeping the arch span the same there

would be no thrust on the piers, so the piers could be greatly reduced in thickness. In order to maintain the stability of the piers during construction, the centering for all arches was erected and the arches built simultaneously, working from the piers towards the crown of the arch to minimise any thrust on the piers. The principal advantages were that the ratio of pier width to arch span could be significantly reduced, thus providing less of an obstruction to river flows, and the arch profiles could be made much flatter. Alexander Nimmo, the designer

GLENDERG BRIDGE, COUNTY TYRONE

The profile of this seven-arch bridge is flat, by comparison with many hump-backed bridges of the period. With spans of up to 20ft, Glenderg Bridge in County Tyrone has been dated as early 18th century. The arch ring is unusual in being constructed of thin sections of largely undressed stone. The regular spacing of the patress plates, and their being set low on the rings, would suggest that these may have been inserted during construction and not at a later stage – a suggestion supported by the fact that the faces of the bridge show no obvious signs of movement.

VARTRY BRIDGE, COUNTY WICKLOW

The normally drowned remains of an abandoned road bridge spanning the Vartry River in County Wicklow and uncovered during drought conditions at the Vartry Reservoir. The rubble stone arches appear to have been well formed. The right-hand arch has partially collapsed at a later stage due to movement of the abutment due to continuing erosion.

GREEN'S BRIDGE,
COUNTY KILKENNY

Spanning the River Nore in Kilkenny, Green's Bridge was erected around 1765 to replace an earlier bridge washed away in the severe floods of 1763. The bridge has been likened to one at Rimini in Italy and the architect, George Smith, certainly attempted to endow the structure with some classical features, such as the pedimented aedicules over each of the piers. The vegetation seen in the photograph, which commonly gains a hold in mortared joints, has recently been cleared.

VICTORIA BRIDGE,
COUNTY KILDARE

An unusual form of cutwater employed by the designer on the piers of the Victoria Bridge spanning the River Liffey in County Kildare. This 19th century bridge provides a good example of the use of ashlar masonry.

of Sarsfield Bridge at Limerick, drew his inspiration from one of Perronet's most famous bridges, the Pont Neuilly over the River Seine in Paris (opened 1772). Nimmo's bridge is now of some historical importance following the replacement of the Parisian bridge in 1956.

In the 1760s, many of the bridges spanning the Rivers Nore and Barrow in County Kilkenny were destroyed or badly damaged by severe floods. George Smith designed replacement structures under an Inland Navigation Act of 1765. He was greatly influenced by the works of

Palladio and this can clearly be seen in the decorations applied to the piers and spandrels of a number of his bridges. In 1776 George Semple published his seminal treatise on building in water, one of the classics of eighteenth century civil engineering literature.

Only three masonry arch bridges in Ireland have single spans equal to or greater than 100ft. A landmark in the construction of masonry arch bridges in Ireland was the bridge at Lismore, completed in 1775. It was not until 1794 that the Lismore span was exceeded in Ireland and

CLARA VALE BRIDGE, COUNTY WICKLOW

Built around 1700, Clara Vale Bridge, spanning the Avonmore River in County Wicklow, serves a route from Laragh to Rathdrum. The six spans of this narrow stone bridge range from 14ft to 21ft, the arch rings being constructed of thin slabs of locally occurring mica schist. The coping of the parapets is also made of the same material with the slabs laid at an angle of 70° to the horizontal. The spandrel walls and piers were built using random rubble (field stone), a method often employed by local masons to build bridges in rural Ireland. The triangular section cutwaters are also typical of early bridges.

then by only a few feet by Sarah's Bridge at Islandbridge in Dublin with a span of 104ft 5in. The last of this trio was the bridge erected in 1814 at Lucan with a span of 110ft. It remains the largest in the country, but still small in comparison to say the 200ft arch at Chester in England. The segmental arches of the two Dublin bridges have a rise to span ratio of 0.2, whereas that at Lismore is 0.29. The ability to span a river with a single arch, provided

RATHDRUM VIADUCT, COUNTY WICKLOW

This stone arch railway viaduct across the Avonmore River at Rathdrum in County Wicklow carries the line from Dublin to Wexford. This photograph, taken around 1860, shows clearly the method of construction of such viaducts. Timber centering (temporary support) has been erected simultaneously for all arches. This technique, first introduced in France in the 18th century, enables the piers to be made much thinner. When all the arches are complete, all the centering is struck at the same time, thus allowing the horizontal thrust of each arch to be counteracted by the opposing thrust of the adjacent arches, until resisted by the abutments.

BROWNSBARN BRIDGE, COUNTY KILKENNY

One of a number of bridges spanning the River Nore in County Kilkenny rebuilt around 1765 by George Smith of the Nore Navigation Board following the devastating flood of 1763. Brownsbarn Bridge has three main spans and four flood arches, giving the bridge a total length of over 460ft.

INISTIOGE BRIDGE, COUNTY KILKENNY

George Smith, following the disastrous floods of 1763, carried out the rebuilding of the bridge across the River Nore at Inistioge in County Kilkenny. He applied the concept of Mylne's design for Blackfriars Bridge in London to the downstream face and the sprandrel walls over the piers are decorated with pairs of Ionic columns using a pale sharp-edged granite. The spandrels themselves are built of good quality dark-coloured rubble stone. All nine arches are equal in span and semi-circular in profile resulting in a parapet that is horizontal rather than rising towards the centre of the bridge.

suitable foundations could be found for the abutments, reduced the risk of scour and the cost of construction and maintenance. However, the increase in span with an associated large rise in an arch, created a new problem, that of excessive gradients on the approaches to the central arch or arches. This problem was overcome in large measure by the use of flatter segmental arches.

Bridges designed in the Gothic style with pointed arches are rare, but that by Nimmo at Poulaphuca in County Wicklow (1820) and by Killaly near Lisdoonvarna in County Clare (1824) are worthy of mention. Of similar design are Ringsend Bridge in Dublin (1812), and the Causeway Bridge at Dungarvan in County Waterford (1816); both have spandrel walls built as radial extensions of the voissoirs. The profile of the arch ring at Ringsend (like Sarsfield in Limerick) is hydraulically efficient, but the masonry is continued across the bed of the river to protect the bridge against the scouring action of the river's flow.

CLARKE'S BRIDGE, COUNTY CORK

Clarke's Bridge was erected in 1766 by Thomas Hobbs, a local carpenter, and was the longest span stone arch in Ireland, until exceeded by Thomas Ivory's arch at Lismore in County Waterford, built some ten years later. The 68ft span bridge crosses the southern channel of the River Lee in Cork city and is subjected daily to modern traffic loading. The arch rings are composed of thin slabs of stone that increase in length towards the abutments. Hobbs managed to avoid having the steep approaches of many contemporary bridges and his design was quite daring for the time.

ATHY BRIDGE, COUNTY KILDARE

This Palladian-style bridge, spanning the River Barrow at Athy in County Kildare, was sponsored by the Duke of Leinster and most probably designed by the engineers of the Barrow Navigation. A plaque on the bridge records the fact that it was built in 1796 by "Sir James Delehunty, Knight of the Trowel", indicating the involvement of a master mason. The bridge is known locally as Croomaboo Bridge, the name coming from 'Crom-a Boo', the war cry of the Desmonds.

GRAIGUENAMANAGH BRIDGE,
COUNTY CARLOW

GRAIGUENAMANAGH BRIDGE,
COUNTY CARLOW

The central arch of the 18th century bridge over the River Barrow at Graiguenamanagh in County Carlow. The influence of Palladio's architectural ideas is evident from the addition of the pedimented aedicules over the flanking piers.

As far as the dating of Ireland's considerable inheritance of stone bridges is concerned, the destruction of the bulk of the Grand Jury records in the Public Record Office during the Civil War in 1922, has left a void in information relating to bridges built and, even more importantly, repaired, in Ireland during the period 1700-1898. Style can act as a guide but can rarely be relied on totally. A local style may suit the stone, funds and skills available and may thus be continued after other styles have been adopted elsewhere. What records remain are

unfortunately very sparse and, without a continuous record, it is not always clear whether a bridge shown, for example on Moll's map of 1714, is that which one sees on the site today. Moll's map is one of the best early sources of information as it covers all Ireland, but it only embraces the 'principal' roads. Thus, the fact that an old looking bridge appears on a secondary road, but not on Moll's map, is not conclusive evidence of a date post-1714. Moll's

SARAH'S BRIDGE, DUBLIN

Located near Kilmainham in Dublin at or near the sites of early medieval fords, the first bridge spanning the River Liffey here dates from the 13th century. This (probably timber) bridge was replaced in 1578 with a multi-span stone arch bridge that lasted until around 1784. The present Sarah's Bridge was designed and built by the elder Alexander Stephens, a noted contractor, considered by Rennie to be 'one of the best.' The single ashlar masonry arch spans 104ft 5in with a rise of 21ft 7in. Following completion in 1794, it remained the longest span in Ireland until exceeded by another fine arch bridge upstream at Lucan in 1814.

AGIVEY BRIDGE, COUNTY DERRY

Agivey Bridge, over the Lower Bann in County Derry, is at least the fourth bridge on the site. A six-span timber bridge designed by William Bald is illustrated in the Second Report on Public Works, Ireland (1834). Under construction in 1833, it replaced a timber bridge of 1795. In 1860, a through latticed girder bridge, with one movable span, was constructed by Victor Coates & Co. of Belfast in wrought-iron with cast-iron piers. This company made machinery at their Lagan foundry and Agivey was their only known bridge. In 1982, a three-span through Warren girder bridge, with outside footpaths, was erected on the existing foundations using standard British Steel sections.

BONDS BRIDGE, COUNTY TYRONE

This iron bridge, over the River Blackwater near Moy in County Tyrone, is of the bowstring girder type. It is made of light sections and marked "Alexe Finlay & Co. Contractors Motherwell Bonds Bridge 1895". With a centre-to-centre span of 105ft, the bridge is only 16ft wide and thus currently carries a 6 tonne weight limit. The under-deck is made up of U sections with flanges, bolted together, whilst the girders on the approach span are marked "Middlesbro", both suggesting the use of steel. The bowstring girders are strengthened against buckling by cross beams on the top chord and the girders are supported on cast-iron columns.

KNOCKLOFTY BRIDGE, COUNTY TIPPERARY

This accommodation bridge for farm vehicles and livestock spans 140ft across the River Suir in the Knocklofty House demesne in County Tipperary. Erected around 1877, to gain access to a new residence being built on the opposite side of the river, the main girders are double latticed with a curved top chord. The bridge is about 16ft wide and the deck is carried on small girders spanning transversely between the bottom flanges of the main girders. The original teak decking was replaced about 1994. The construction of this privately funded bridge must have represented a considerable challenge and investment for its promoters.

THOMASTOWN VIADUCT, COUNTY KILKENNY

The main span of the original railway viaduct across the River Nore at Thomastown in County Kilkenny, formed of timber latticed girders, was replaced in 1877 by twin bowstring wrought-iron girders spanning 212ft. Designed by C R Galwey and manufactured by the Dublin firm of Courtney, Stephens and Bailey, the web of each girder is divided into fifteen equal bays by diagonal bracing and has stiffening plates at the ends. The main span is approached by pairs of masonry arches, the central piers of which incorporate transverse relieving arches.

GREENISLAND VIADUCT, COUNTY ANTRIM

At the time of its construction in 1933, the soaring concrete viaduct at Greenisland in County Antrim was the largest reinforced concrete railway project in either Britain or Ireland. The Belfast & Ballymena Railway (by 1923, the LMS NCC) suffered from having an indirect line to Antrim. The opportunity afforded by unemployment relief legislation was taken to remedy this. The viaduct, nine approach spans of 35ft and three main spans of 83ft, carries the double main line by a direct route. A second viaduct with one main span carries the down line to Larne. Built by direct labour, much of the design was undertaken by the railway company who engaged F A MacDonald of Glasgow as consultant.

ATHY RAIL, COUNTY KILDARE

In 1918, the Great Southern & Western Railway laid a branch to Wolfhill Collieries near Athy in County Kildare. This crosses the River Barrow on a six-span reinforced concrete bridge and continues to carry regular freight traffic to a nearby factory. Longitudinal beams, 2ft thick and 5ft 9in. deep, support cross beams extended under the concrete parapet as cantilevers. The piers are carried up as solid sections. Whilst the deck layout is typical of the period, the piers are not. This is the earliest major concrete rail under-bridge in Ireland, but several smaller under-bridges on the former LMS NCC railway in Northern Ireland date from 1913.

KINGS BRIDGE, BELFAST

The designer of the Kings Bridge in Belfast was selected by the City Corporation in open competition. Three entries were received, that of the Trussed Steel Concrete Co. being accepted. Patent Kahn bars, intended to give improved bond and shear protection, were used. The design arrangement is conventional beam and slab, with 4ft 3in deep longitudinal beams. There are four spans, two of 40ft and two of 50ft. The River Lagan flows here on soft silts and the bridge has foundation problems; it now carries a 7.5 tonne weight limit. Furthermore, the Harbour Commissioners dictated that it be placed at right angles to the navigation to facilitate barge traffic, since ceased. A replacement skew bridge is proposed.

EAST LODGE BRIDGE, CORK

This 60ft span reinforced concrete segmental arch bridge gives access across a channel of the River Lee to the campus of University College Cork. It was built 1928-30 to replace an earlier two-span concrete beam and slab structure erected in 1913. The local designer of the present East Lodge Bridge, B.O'Flynn, employed the Coignet system of reinforcement and the contractor was J.Murphy of Cork. Due to the steep dip of the limestone escarpment on which the college is situated, the piles for the northern abutment had to be driven down to a depth three times that estimated, which led to severe cost escalation.

FOYLE BRIDGE,
COUNTY DERRY

A new link to the north-west and County Donegal was established with the opening of the Foyle Bridge near Londonderry in 1984. Navigation requirements necessitated a clearance of 32m over a width of 130m. The main span of 233m, the largest in Ireland, consists of twin steel box girders, fabricated by Harland and Wolff of Belfast, and transported by sea to the site. Side spans are each 144m. The curving approach to the bridge from the east is over five spans of pre-stressed concrete box girders. Designers were Ove Arup & Partners and the bridge was built by a consortium of Redpath Dorman Long, Grahams of Dromore and Freeman Fox & Partners.

MIZEN HEAD FOOTBRIDGE,
COUNTY CORK

The 1909 footbridge to Mizen Head lighthouse off the west coast of County Cork spans a 150ft deep sea inlet. Access was difficult and the problem of how to erect the bridge was solved by pre-casting the arch ribs in four pieces on shore. A cableway was suspended across the inlet and the pieces swung into place and fixed in position. The arch then provided access for the casting in situ of the deck, its supports and cross-bracing. This method of construction was highly innovative for 1989. The bridge, spanning 172ft, was designed to the Ridley & Cammell system using one inch flat reinforcing bars and built by Alfred Thorne & Son of London.

ROCKINGHAM BRIDGE, COUNTY ROSCOMMON

Rockingham Bridge spans the N4 (Curlew Mountains section) and links Boyle in County Roscommon with Lough Key Forest Park. The scenic and high amenity nature of the area, a nearby arch structure and the ground conditions at the site, led the consultants, Molloy Pollock Punch, to select a reinforced concrete open spandrel arch bridge that sits well in the deep cutting, the repeated 'gothic' arch design on the parapets intending to enhance the appearance of the bridge. The contractor was the Western Division of SIAC Construction.

MAURICE O'NEILL MEMORIAL BRIDGE, COUNTY KERRY

Designed by Ralph Ryan of the Galway based Ryan Hanley partnership, this substantial pre-stressed beam and slab road bridge connects Valentia Island with the mainland at Portmagee in County Kerry. The superstructure is supported on bored concrete piles taken down to the bedrock. The bridge, which was built by contractor P.J. Hegarty, was named the Maurice O'Neill Memorial Bridge when opened in 1970.

DEVERNEY BRIDGE, COUNTY TYRONE

Deverney Bridge in County Tyrone was completed in 1931 to replace an arch bridge washed away two years previously. It consists of a central span of 55ft 6in., flanked on either side by flat-soffit spans of 20ft to allow for the passage of floodwater. The reinforced concrete bridge carries a minor road across the Camowen River. The deck over the arch is supported directly off four parallel longitudinal arch ribs, rather than having the more usual beam and slab arrangement supported solely off the side arch ribs.

CAHIRCIVEEN ROAD VIADUCT, COUNTY KERRY

This long narrow beam and slab reinforced concrete road viaduct was completed in the 1930s to connect the town of Cahirciveen in County Kerry with a network of minor roads on a peninsula on the opposite side of the estuary of the Valentia River. The designer reused the masonry abutments and piers of an earlier structure. The building with the mock Scottish baronial tower at the south-east end of the bridge provides it with a unique setting.

KENMARE BRIDGE, COUNTY KERRY

Kenmare Bridge in County Kerry replaces a twin-span suspension bridge that had one central pier founded on a rock islet in the estuary and erected 1840. The 1933 replacement bridge has two concrete arches, 157ft span and 31ft wide, in the style of the Sydney Harbour Bridge, opened the previous year. The arches, springing from the top of the original central pier, are 2ft 6in. thick and taper from 4ft 9in. to 3ft; hangers off the arch carry the transverse beams forming the deck. Design was undertaken by Mouchel & Partners with specialist advice from Professor Pierce Purcell, and the contractor was A. E. Farr of London.

HARTLEY BRIDGE, COUNTY LEITRIM

Mizen Head used one of the early patent concrete reinforcing systems, Hartley Bridge in County Leitrim, opened in 1915, uses another. This was the patent of William Moss & Son that used a rail section and links in the form of a triangle. Here, the parapet is structural, forming a 4ft deep beam, the maximum span being 60ft across the navigation channel. The deck spans to the underside, thus forming a trough or U-shaped section. Piers and bracing are lightweight, suggesting that most of the load is carried directly by the rail sections. Moss provided the design for Leitrim County Council and the bridge was erected under the supervision of the county engineer's office using direct labour.

CAUSEWAY BRIDGE, COUNTY WATERFORD

The building of the Causeway Bridge at Dungarvan in County Waterford formed part of the improvements to the town carried out at the beginning of the 19th century by the Dukes of Devonshire of Lismore Castle. The segmental arch bridge, spanning 77ft 6in. across the mouth of the River Colligan, was built with sandstone imported from Cheshire, rather than the local occurring limestone. The joints in the spandrel walls are radial, being a continuation of the voussoir joints, thus creating a pleasing fan-shaped appearance. Construction work was supervised between 1809 and 1816 by the Yorkshire born civil engineer, Jesse Hartley.

LISMORE BRIDGE, COUNTY WATERFORD

The 5th Duke of Devonshire commissioned the first stone bridge across the River Blackwater at Lismore in County Waterford. When completed in 1779, the single arch of 100 ft over the main channel of the river was the longest in Ireland. Built by Darley and Stokes to a design by Thomas Ivory, the bridge is approached across the flood plain of the river by a viaduct of eight spans, rebuilt in 1858. An unusual feature of the bridge is that the springing point of the main arch at the north abutment is over 7 ft below that of the south abutment to accommodate the profile of the river valley at this location.

map is drawn at a small scale and one must question just how accurate the position of the roads are as shown and how much they were sketched to avoid showing many of the bends, which would have make the map unreadable.

For many stone bridges, locally available stone or 'fieldstone' would have been used in their construction. This stone would have been naturally occurring and would have been either

collected or quarried. Depending on the location, limestone, granite or sandstone would have been available, or some local geological variant of these rock types, such as 'greywacke'. Fieldstone was sometimes used in its naturally occurring state, otherwise the stone would have been dressed to fit as required. The stones would generally have only been roughly

SARAH'S BRIDGE, DUBLIN

Close-up view of the northern end of Sarah's Bridge, showing the arch springing from the base of the abutment. The voissoir stones in the arch ring have been hammered to provide a form of restrained decoration. Other detailing to be seen includes the typical Georgian style string course running immediately beneath the parapet.

DAINGEAN CANAL BRIDGE, COUNTY OFFALY

Typical of the many bridges spanning Irish canals, this example, across the Grand Canal at Daingean in County Offaly, has a three-centered or near elliptical style of arch profile, which provides maximum clearance across the waterway for barges and for the horses that towed them.

CANAL BRIDGE, TULLAMORE, COUNTY OFFALY
An attractive canal bridge carrying a local road over the Grand Canal near to its junction with a spur leading to the harbour facilities at Tullamore in County Offaly. The famous Irish engineer John Killaly completed the canal in 1804 from Tullamore to the River Shannon at Shannon Harbour to the north of Banagher in County Offaly.

dressed. For major bridges where sufficient finance was available, good quality stone in large blocks could be quarried, often at some considerable distance from the bridge site, or even from overseas. The stones were dressed by squaring off their faces, and these would be laid in courses. Stone, highly tooled to produce close-fitting blocks with very thin joints, is referred to as 'ashlar'.

Joints in the stonework are normally filled with mortar. The lime mortar used in early stone bridges presented two difficulties - it was very slow to set and the strength could not always be relied on. The slow set made the mortar vulnerable to being washed out by flowing water or rain. To ensure good quality quick lime, the limestone had to be raised to a sufficiently high temperature to drive off sufficient carbon dioxide and this could not always be guaranteed.

RYEWATER BRIDGE, CARTON ESTATE,
COUNTY KILDARE

This Palladian style bridge, also known as the 'Classical Bridge', is a graceful multi-arched structure spanning a placid ornamental lake in the grounds of Carton in County Kildare. It is believed that the design of the bridge was based on one by Isaac Ware, and that the architect Thomas Ivory may have supervised its construction. The pointed cutwaters on the piers seem unnecessary for such a situation.

However, good quality well-set lime mortar is a strong and durable substance. When cements first became available, they were sometimes used for jointing (and in the mass in foundations) below water level, whilst lime mortar was used above.

In order for an arch to remain stable, the line of thrust must lie within the so-called middle third of the arch ring. If it passes outside of the middle third, tensile stress develops, which

O'DONOVAN ROSSA BRIDGE, DUBLIN

The present bridge was erected 1813-16 to replace one located nearby that had been carried away by a flood. The bridge, with three segmental arches, each of an average span of 44ft, and built of Wicklow granite, was designed by James Savage and built by George Knowles. A particular feature is the heads carved on the keystones; those on the downstream face represent Plenty, Anna Livia and Industry, whilst those on the upstream face represent Commerce, Hibernia and Peace. With its balustraded parapets and well-proportioned arches, O'Donovan Rossa Bridge forms an important part of the architectural fabric of Dublin.

WHITWORTH AQUEDUCT, COUNTY LONGFORD

The Whitworth Aqueduct carries the Royal Canal over the River Inny near Abbeyshrule in County Longford. It was designed by the talented Irish canal engineer, John Killaly, and constructed between 1814 and 1817 by the leading firm of Irish contractors, Henry, Mullins and MacMahon. To improve stability, the spandrel walls are splayed outwards, thus increasing the width of the canal foundations. The waterway at this point is 15ft 6in. wide at the water level reducing to 13ft wide at the base. There are 8ft wide towpaths on either side of the canal. The final stretch of the canal from Dublin is currently being restored and it is hoped to be able to complete the restoration of the navigation to the Shannon within the near future.

BALLYSKEAGH HIGH BRIDGE, COUNTY DOWN

The old main road from Belfast to Lisburn crossed the River Lagan at Drum in County Down, proceeding by Hillhall to Hillsborough. A more direct route diverged at Drum, passing over Wolfenden's Bridge. When the Lagan Navigation was constructed, the river at this point was bypassed and a deep cutting constructed at Ballyskeagh. The road was carried on a bridge, known as the High Bridge, due to its tall arches of sandstone blocks, and completed about 1760. Another local tradition has it that the last person executed in Ulster for sheep stealing was hung from the bridge, but it has been suggested that linen stealing was a more likely offence.

may cause instability. During construction, however, for the process known as 'the turning of the arch', considerable temporary falsework is needed to support the weight of the material used to make up the arch. In brick construction, the arch may be built up from a number of rings of brickwork.

SPECTACLE BRIDGE,
COUNTY CLARE

In 1875, the County Surveyor of
County Clare, John Hill, was faced
with the problem of carrying the
Ennistymon to Lisdoonvarna in
County Clare road over a narrow river
gorge, at places up to 80ft deep. To avoid
excessively deep spandrel walls, he provided
an ordinary semicircular masonry arch at low
level. Resting on this he constructed
masonry brickwork to form a large circular
opening, on top of which the roadway was
carried. The visual effect from river level
gave rise to the name Spectacle Bridge.

There are a number of ways in which an arch may fail, including development of excessive tensile stress in the jointing material, development of excessive compressive stress in the jointing material, sliding of one voussoir over another, and spreading of the abutments. Other possibilities are failure of the foundation, fracture of the stone, or an arch may simply be overturned by the force of the floodwaters.

ATHLUNKARD BRIDGE, LIMERICK

Built between 1826 and 1830 under the direction of the Directors General of Inland Navigation to provide a new route northwards from Limerick city, the bridge over the River Shannon at Athlunkard was designed by the architectural firm of J.& G.R.Pain. The Pains were pupils of the famous London architect, John Nash. The bridge, built to withstand the severest floods, has five segmental arches each of 67ft span, 30ft thick abutments and piers around 10ft thick, the substantial curved cutwaters offering protection from floating debris. An attractive tollhouse (now a private dwelling) exists nearby.

SCARIFF BRIDGE, COUNTY MEATH

Drainage works on the River Boyne, carried out under an Act of 1849, necessitated, in several instances, the realignment of the riverbed and the replacement or partial removal of a number of multi-span stone bridges. Scariff Bridge in County Meath, designed by the engineers of the Office of Public Works, is a single arch having a span of 60ft and a rise of only 9ft. The absence of piers maximises the hydraulic flow capacity of the river. The bridge has radial joints in the spandrel walls as a continuation of the voissoir joints.

FEALE BRIDGE, COUNTY LIMERICK

In 1822 Richard Griffith was sent by the government to the southwest of Ireland to open up communications with the more remote districts. Griffith designed Feale Bridge in County Limerick as a single masonry arch bridge of 70ft span to replace an ageing stone bridge with no less than twenty-one small arches. The river was notable for its flash floods and there was thus the need to provide secure foundations for the bridge abutments. The elliptical profile of the arch also aids flood discharge.

The jointing material used, depending on its nature, may offer some resistance to tensile stress. This results in an increased loading range, because the line of thrust can lie outside the middle third. A good lime mortar will easily resist the tensile stress applied to it under normal conditions of loading. The condition of the fill above the arch ring also influences the overall strength of the structure.

SYNOD HALL FOOTBRIDGE, DUBLIN

The substantial footbridge connecting Christ Church Cathedral with the Synod Hall across St Michael's Hill in Dublin was completed around 1875. It was designed by the English Gothic Revivalist architect, George Edmund Street, who is said to have derived his inspiration from the "Bridge of Sighs" in Venice. The bridge was built in a First Pointed or early Gothic style with relatively simple arcades lining the walls. Four masonry arch ribs, each of 35ft span, are spanned transversely by stone slabs. The arch in turn supports the arcade, which contains a descending stairway allowing movements between the two buildings.

Accurate methods for assessing the strength of masonry arches are of particular importance given the very large number of such structures that are still in service in Ireland. Such assessment is complicated by the wide variety of arch types and the considerable differences in their methods and quality of construction. The term masonry arch encompasses both early stone arch bridges and the highly engineered masonry arches constructed during the nineteenth century.

CRAIGMORE VIADUCT, COUNTY DOWN

The stone viaduct near Newry in County Down carrying the main line between Dublin and Belfast over the Camlough river valley is, at 139ft, the tallest railway bridge in Ireland. Designed by Sir John Macneill and built by William Dargan, the Craigmore Viaduct, which is on a slight curve at its northern end, has eighteen semicircular arches, each of about 59 ft 6 in. span. The piers are 7ft 6in. thick at springing level and the width of the track way is 28ft. The stone used was local Newry grano-diorite. The viaduct was opened to traffic on 13 May 1852.

Where it is considered necessary to extend the life of a masonry bridge on an important transportation route, major rehabilitation has often been undertaken. In many instances this has led to the sprandrel walls being stabilised by being injected with liquid cement (grouting) and the arch soffits sprayed with layers of liquid concrete (guniting). This treatment alters the way in which the bridge was designed to act under load and tends to convert the multi-arch bridge into a monolithic structure little different to a solid causeway with openings. The original aesthetically pleasing outward appearance of many such rehabilitated structures has, however, often been retained. ❖

BILLA BRIDGE,
COUNTY SLIGO

Billa Bridge spans the Owenbeg River near Ballysodare in County Sligo. This single 36ft span masonry arch bridge was erected in 1887 at the expense of the local cesspayers (ratepayers) together with a contribution from a local landlord, C.W. O'Hara of Annaghmore. The designer was the County Surveyor, C.B. Jones. It is sometimes known as the 'wriggle' bridge due to the parapets being continued in both directions along the curving approach road, so giving the bridge the appearance of an 'S' shape in plan.

CHAPTER FOUR
METAL BRIDGES

Metal Bridges

etal bridges, generally of iron or steel, are less common in Ireland than in the industrialised areas of Britain. Primarily, this is because there was locally available stone and brick suitable for use for bridgework, whilst metal was generally more expensive or had to be imported. The perfection of the process, whereby elements could be formed of cast iron in a mould, soon resulted in the construction of cast-iron

BALLYDUFF UPPER BRIDGE,
COUNTY WATERFORD

bridges. A certain quantity of pig iron was imported and fashioned into bridge parts by small Irish foundries and such bridges may carry the mark of the local foundry concerned.

The first major bridge structure in metal was Iron Bridge in Shropshire, opened on New Year's Day 1781 and still standing. The bridge has an arch made up of a series of parallel circular ribs, the whole braced together radially and horizontally. Parts of the arch ribs were

LIFFEY BRIDGE (HA'PENNY BRIDGE), DUBLIN

The Liffey (or Ha'penny) footbridge, a Dublin icon erected in 1816, is the oldest metal arch bridge in Ireland. It is generally accepted that the design was by John Windsor, a foreman at Abraham Darby III's iron foundry at Coalbrookdale in Shropshire, this foundry having, in 1781, supplied the castings for the first successful iron bridge, erected over the River Severn. The bridge at Dublin was cast in eighteen sections and later bolted together on site to form the cast-iron ribs spanning 138ft across the river. An extensive refurbishment of the bridge has been completed and the bridge reopened on 21st December 2001. Some ten million pedestrians cross this landmark heritage structure every year.

BENVARDIN BRIDGE, COUNTY ANTRIM

Several ornate bridges resulted from the Victorian vogue for perambulating demesne gardens. Benvardin, over the River Bush near Dervock in County Antrim, is a fine example. Like the Chetwynd Viaduct, south west of Cork, the spandrels are infilled with diagonal latticework. The main span, 14ft wide and sufficient for a horse-drawn carriage, is 55ft. The metalwork has no casting marks but was reputedly cast in Dublin. The present owner possesses a drawing showing the requirements for end recesses, indicating that the fine stonework abutments and approach spans were designed and built locally. There is a tradition that several estate farms were sold to pay for the bridge.

cast in sections and the whole pegged together with iron wedges. As iron foundry technology continued to advance, bridge elements were soon being cast in larger sections. By the time of the erection of the Liffey (or Ha'penny) Bridge in Dublin (erected 1816), the six large castings forming each of the three ribs could be bolted together and cross-braced.

In England, the failure in 1817 of Coalport Bridge (erected 1799) and in 1899 of Telford's Bridge (erected 1796) highlighted a major difficulty with cast iron - it is very strong in compression but weak in tension. To overcome this difficulty with the material, cast-iron bridges were soon being built of two large sections cantilevered from either side and meeting at the centre or simply supporting a mid section. The I-section solid cantilevers were deep at the abutments and these bridges generally exhibit a massive appearance. To reduce the dead weight, the webs of the cantilever beams were frequently pierced by openings; these were

BARRINGTON BRIDGE, COUNTY LIMERICK

Although completed in 1818, just two years after the Liffey Bridge, and thus historically significant, Barrington Bridge, located to the south-east of Limerick, is much less well known. Here, the design concept is also markedly different. Nine internal ribs, cross-tied to the arch members, and formed of bolted flanged 12in. diameter cast-iron pipes, support the roadway. The spandrels of the outer solid cast-iron arch members are neatly ornamented. The cost of construction was borne by Sir Matthew Barrington, who owned estates in the area. This important part of Ireland's infrastructural heritage has been preserved, a new concrete bridge having been installed alongside to accommodate the increased traffic using the route.

often rectangular as at Lough Atalia, but other shapes will be noticed. Gradually, the solid webs of the cantilevers were replaced with flower-like openings or by much lighter forms, such as the interlocked arches seen on the remains of the bridge by Bairds of Glasgow at Muckamore in County Antrim (1822), circles or Xs, as at Benvardin in County Antrim, Oak Park in County Carlow and Chetwynd south-west of Cork. On these bridges, the deck is carried on the top of the cantilevered girders.

Apart from being strong in compression and weak in tension, cast iron has good corrosion properties but is quite brittle. The casting process can result in flaws in the metal or holes

('blows'), both of which weaken the final result. Working the iron to drive out the impurities and to reduce the carbon content led to the production of wrought iron, which is stronger in tension. However, it corrodes more easily than cast iron, but generally not as quickly as the various types of modern steel.

ALBERT BRIDGE, BELFAST

The Albert Bridge in Belfast is a good example of late Victorian cast-iron work. The bridge was opened in 1890 to replace one that collapsed in 1886. Prince Albert Victor laid the foundation stone. There are three flat segmental arches, each 85 ft span and consisting of eleven cast-iron ribs with intermediate stiffeners. The bridge abutments are granite-faced brickwork. The contractor was James Henry & Sons, and A Handyside & Co of Derby supplied the castings to a general design by the City Surveyor, J. C. Bretland. The deck has recently been strengthened and the details on the bridge highlighted using contrasting coloured paint.

LOUGH ATALIA RAIL BRIDGE, GALWAY

As the weight of railway trains increased, so cast-iron bridges became more massive in form. However, the material in the spandrels is structurally under-utilised. Attempts were made to reduce the total weight of the structure by piercing the spandrels as here in the side span of the rail bridge at Lough Atalia, which crosses an approach road to Galway City. Erected for the Midland Great Western Railway, the 32ft span, which contains twenty ribs in its width of close on 100 ft, is marked "James Stephens, Iron Works, Galway" at each end of the arch.

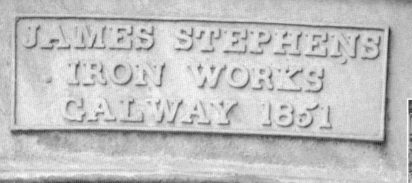

**FOUNDRY PLATE, LOUGH ITALIA
RAILWAY BRIDGE, GALWAY**
Plate on side span of Lough Italia railway bridge in
Galway providing details of the casting foundry.

**OAK PARK BRIDGE,
COUNTY CARLOW**
This elegant cast-iron estate bridge was erected in 1818 on the Oak
Park demesne near Carlow and spans the outlet from an artificial
lake. The bridge elements were cast, like those for the Liffey
Bridge in Dublin, at the Coalbrookedale foundry in Shropshire.
The massive abutments, between which the cast-iron ribs were
set, and the overall design is believed to be that of the architect
George Papworth. Oak Park Bridge is of international
significance, only very few of its type having survived the ravages
of time.

**FOUNDRY MARK,
SHANNONBRIDGE,
COUNTY OFFALY**
Mark of J & R Mallet Founders Dublin cast on one of the
preserved leaves of the original swivel bridge at Shannonbridge
in County Offaly.

The production of wrought iron I-beams, originally intended for the fireproof construction
of mill buildings, allowed for the construction of bridges with longitudinal arches of brick
resting on an extended bottom flange of cast- or wrought-iron beams. Locally made brick was
more readily available than iron, making this form of construction attractive. This
arrangement is known as 'jack arching'. Bridges of this design, however, tend to be weak. To
stop the beams moving sideways, tie rods run from side to side. All too often, these cannot

be inspected (being partly within the brick) and, if sufficient rusting takes place, these can fail suddenly. Few brick jack-arch bridges have therefore survived, but an unaltered example may still be seen at Seafin in County Down, erected in 1878.

In the early years of railway transportation, long spans presented great difficulty. One solution, developed by William Fairbairn and Robert Stephenson in the mid 19th century for the crossing of the Menai straits in North Wales, was to form a large metal tube, or box girder, through which the rail traffic passed. There are no examples of this through type of large box

CHETWYND VIADUCT, COUNTY CORK

Built in 1851 for the Cork and Bandon Railway to a design by Charles Nixon, a pupil of the famous engineer Isambard Kingdom Brunel, Chetwynd Viaduct has four spans each of 110 ft providing headroom of 83ft. The cast-iron sections were supplied and erected by a leading English company, Fox Henderson. The arch ribs would have been transported to the site in sections, bolted together and lifted into preformed recesses in the abutments. The ribs are braced transversely and the arch spandrels are latticed. The photograph, taken around 1890, shows a portion of the viaduct in its original condition, the appearance having been subsequently. Extra bracing was added over the piers and, following closure of the railway, the bridge deck was removed.

girder in Ireland, but smaller box girders were used for the Suir Viaduct at Cahir in County Tipperary. Here, pairs of box girders were used to span between the piers and cross beams, or stringers, used to support the rail tracks. Smaller examples, such as the three-span rail bridge carrying the Dublin-Galway line across the River Suck at Ballinasloe in County Galway, or the bridge carrying a 'shaugh' (small stream) over the former Lisburn to Banbridge line at

WELLINGTONBRIDGE STATION FOOTBRIDGE, COUNTY WEXFORD

An example of the Victorian style footbridges provided by railway companies to allow passengers to cross the line at stations in safety. That at Wellingtonbridge station in County Wexford was supplied from the Dundalk foundry of E.Manisty. Very few of these bridges remain and maintenance is essential to keep them in good order.

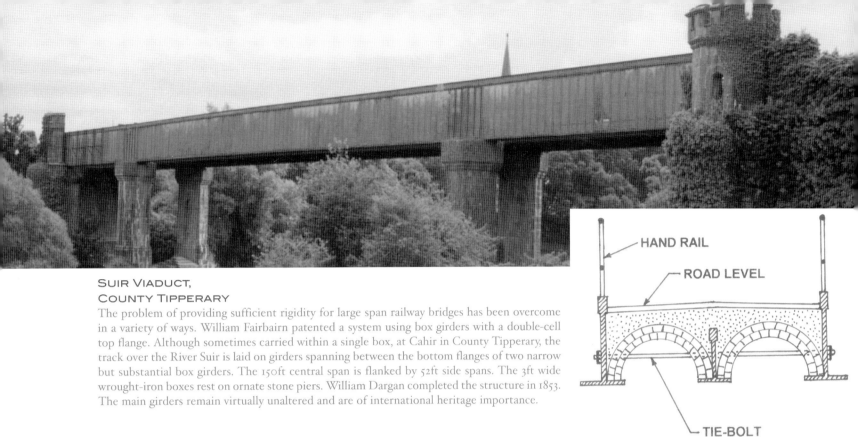

SUIR VIADUCT, COUNTY TIPPERARY

The problem of providing sufficient rigidity for large span railway bridges has been overcome in a variety of ways. William Fairbairn patented a system using box girders with a double-cell top flange. Although sometimes carried within a single box, at Cahir in County Tipperary, the track over the River Suir is laid on girders spanning between the bottom flanges of two narrow but substantial box girders. The 150ft central span is flanked by 52ft side spans. The 3ft wide wrought-iron boxes rest on ornate stone piers. William Dargan completed the structure in 1853. The main girders remain virtually unaltered and are of international heritage importance.

HAND RAIL

ROAD LEVEL

TIE-BOLT

SECTION OF JACK ARCHES

Hillsborough in County Down, may also be noticed. Within the past twenty-five years, there has been a resurgence of interest in box-girder design in steel or pre-stressed concrete, but with the boxes situated below the deck.

The production of wrought-iron allowed the construction of large latticed girders, such as those used on the Boyne Rail Viaduct of 1855 near Drogheda, and the construction of trusses. Trusses capable of bridging long spans were developed, largely in America. The general arrangement was to

FOUNDRY PLATE, WELLINGTONBRIDGE, COUNTY WEXFORD.
Manisty's foundry plate on the footbridge at Wellingtonbridge in County Wexford.

cross-brace these at the bottom members such that traffic passed between the side trusses (the 'through' layout). Several truss arrangements have been developed and there is a representative selection of them in Ireland.

The Warren truss dates from 1848, but was not favoured on account of its open appearance suggesting a lack of strength. Warren arrangements have recently come back into favour for truss design, but now use steel. Steel is stronger again than wrought iron but is more prone

THOMASTOWN VIADUCT, COUNTY KILKENNY

A railway engine driver's view approaching Thomastown Viaduct in County Kilkenny. The use of rivets to joint the various steel plates, which form the supporting ends of the bowstring trusses are clearly seen. With the rail deck supported at the bottom member of the truss, this constitutes an example of the 'through girder' type of bridge.

CARRICKABRACK VIADUCT, COUNTY CORK

The main span of Carrickabrack Viaduct near Fermoy in County Cork illustrates the 'deck' type of truss arrangement. In this case, a pair of wrought-iron latticed girders support the rail deck along their top chords. An additional lightweight handrail has been added along the side of the railway line. The bridge was designed by James Otway and erected in 1872.

OBELISK BRIDGE, COUNTY MEATH

Obelisk Bridge, in County Meath between Drogheda and Slane, is of the through girder type formed of top and bottom members and double layers of closely spaced diagonal latticing. The bridge was built in 1868, near to the site of the Battle of the Boyne (1690), to replace one in timber washed away in a flood. The clear span of the girders, which rest on rollers on the masonry abutments to allow for expansion, is 120 ft and the girder depth is 1/12 the span. Thomas Grendon & Co. prefabricated the 28-ton wrought-iron girders and floated them on pontoons up the River Boyne from their works at Drogheda to the site.

to corrosion. Agivey Bridge, erected 1982 across the Lower Bann in County Derry was the first, in either Britain or Ireland, to be designed using British Steel standard hollow sections. These are produced in large quantities for building work and were thus readily available. This form of construction has resulted in a significant reduction in dead weight when compared to the wrought-iron trusses previously used.

VERNORS BRIDGE, COUNTY TYRONE/ARMAGH BORDER

Vernors Bridge on the Tyrone/Armagh border is of the through truss type, the trusses being fully braced with cross and vertical elements. It is constructed of steel T- and angle section. It is located where the originally the main road from Portadown to Dungannon crossed the River Blackwater. The approach from Portadown is over deep bog and the road was badly affected by subsidence. It was thus one of the first sections of road to be concreted in the early 1930s, but subsidence continued. The bridge probably dates from the same time. The road was bypassed by an early county section of the Ml motorway, thus preserving the bridge in its present unaltered condition.

The Howe truss was developed for construction in timber, the diagonal members being in compression. Its inverse arrangement, the Pratt truss, was for use in iron, the diagonal members being in tension. There are several examples of the use of Pratt trusses in Ireland. Some late 19th century bridges use a modified form with an extra diagonal member carried down to the end support.

The main bending moment in a truss is at its mid span and some reduction in dead weight was achieved by using the curved top member of the truss, as in the accommodation bridge spanning the River Suir at Knocklofty in County Tipperary. This curved arrangement is known as a bowstring truss. As our understanding of the properties of structural materials improved, bowstring trusses composed of lighter sections became achievable, examples being the Thomastown Viaduct in County Kilkenny and Bond's Bridge in County Tyrone. On a small number of footbridges the curved tension member was placed underneath the deck, which is in compression, a configuration known as an under-slung bowstring truss, Carrick

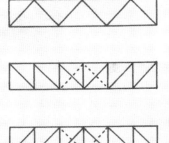

TRUSS TYPES (FROM TOP)
Warren, Pratt, Howe, Modified Pratt, Bowstring and Underslung Trusses.

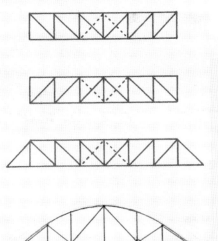

**LAUNE VIADUCT,
COUNTY KERRY**
Laune Viaduct near Killorglin in County Kerry with its three 95ft spans of bowstring girders carried a branch line, which was subsequently extended to Valentia. The use of solid tension members and compression members composed of latticework gives the bridge a delicate appearance. The tapered piers are built of large stone blocks and have round-headed cutwaters. The use of stone was perhaps unusual at a time when cheaper brickwork for railway bridges was becoming common, but local stone probably worked out cheaper. Designed by the Great Southern and Western Railway and erected by T K Falkiner and S G Frazer, the bridge opened in 1885. The line was closed in 1960.

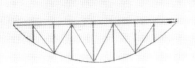

Rocks near Limavady in County Antrim being an example.

Towards the end of the 19th century, the railway companies in particular tended to favour the use of solid plate girders in bridges. These could be brought to site in sections and there riveted or bolted together. Many have been removed with the closure of a large number of railway lines but some remain. Later plate girders were made of steel, especially after it became possible to roll sheets and sections such as angles. Plate girder bridges, although of poor

POULGORM BRIDGE, COUNTY CORK

The 616ft long Poulgorm Bridge spans the upper reaches of the Glandore estuary near Union Hall in County Cork. The 20ft wide deck is supported on piers composed of sets of four 12in. internal diameter cast-iron pipes cross-braced above the waterline, a strong yet economical solution much favoured in late Victorian times. In 1972, Cyril Roche of Cork designed the present arrangement, when a new steel and concrete deck was installed on the 1885 piers. The contractor for the refurbished bridge was John Paul Construction.

aesthetic quality, tend to be cheaper, especially when replacing earlier trusses on existing abutments. They also have a robust appearance, which gave a sense of security to rail passengers.

As was noted in the second chapter, suspension bridges may use chains, single heavy wires or bundled or twisted small diameter wires to form the main cables. In 1836, James Dredge, of Bath, patented his taper principle for suspension bridge construction. The main cable was

CAPPOQUIN RAIL BRIDGE, COUNTY WATERFORD

Multiple-span plate girder structure, typical of those built by the various railway companies in the first quarter of the 20th century to replace earlier light structures in metal or timber. Such replacements were a direct consequence of the use of larger and heavier steam locomotives as the weights of trains increased. The viaduct shown here carried the line from Waterford to Mallow across the River Blackwater at Cappoquin in County Waterford.

PORTUMNA BRIDGE, COUNTY GALWAY

Hayes Island in the River Shannon near Portumna in County Galway was chosen as a crossing point as it allowed for the construction of two shorter structures. The present bridge is an example of a substantial road structure built in solid plate girders. It was built in 1911 to replace one erected in 1834. There are three spans (totalling 260ft) to the east and three on the west (totalling 240ft), the river navigation channel being cut into the riverbank. The supports are 9 ft diameter concrete-filled cast-iron cylinders finished off above parapet level with onion style decorative caps. Designed by C E Stanier, it was built by Hernan and Froude of Manchester.

made up of flat wrought-iron plates. At each deck support, the outermost pair was carried down to the deck, thus acting as an inclined hanger. As a consequence, the cable is thickest at the towers and thinnest at mid span. Few of his bridges remain, but three examples survive in the North of Ireland.

In 1852, an Irishman, Robert Mallet, patented his 'buckled plates' for use in supporting bridge decks. The deck support is made up from a series of square or rectangular plates pressed to a curve in two directions, thereby adding strength to the flat plate. The plates

GLENARB FOOTBRIDGE, COUNTY TYRONE/ARMAGH BORDER

James Dredge's patented taper principle suspension bridges, being made up of small individual pieces, were ideally suited to local manufacture, that shown here at Glenarb on the County Tyrone/Armagh border being cast by the Armagh Foundry in 1844. The Glenarb footbridge, with a main span of 77ft 9in., provided access to Lord Caledon's mill, long since closed. The bridge was refurbished and re-erected in 1990 in its present location to serve as part of a riverside walk.

spanned between I-beams. Buckled plate decks should not be confused with decks supported on transverse radiused metal plates, joined together along their long side and spanning between longitudinal beams on their short side. An example is that used in the Inishmore viaduct on Upper Lough Erne in County Fermanagh (commenced 1891).

Although a number of railway bridges were rebuilt in the early 20th century using plate girders, iron was soon displaced by concrete (apart from one or two larger bridges). Concrete

BALLYSIMON RAILWAY BRIDGE, COUNTY LIMERICK

A view of the underside of the very solid looking railway bridge at Ballysimon in County Limerick. The main structural side members consist of heavy Pratt trusses. The cross-bracing beams to the lower members are clearly seen, the rail tracks being carried on the small-sized longitudinal beams. The formation is carried on curved plates spanning to the crossbeams. The widespread use of rivets and the very appreciable skew on which the Limerick to Limerick Junction railway here crosses the main road to Tipperary are very noticeable.

VALENTIA RIVER VIADUCT, COUNTY KERRY

The railway branch from Killorglin to Valentia in County Kerry was one of the last Irish lines of any significant length to be built and was one of the most heavily engineered. The line, opened in 1893, had a number of bridges and viaducts, including that on a 30° skew over the Valentia River near Cahirciveen. Here, plate girder approach spans on each side of the river lead to the main crossing consisting of seven spans, each of 98ft 6in., of through modified Pratt trusses carried on cast-iron columns.

has advantages in using local sand and stone (and, with the opening of the Irish cement factories, cement) and largely unskilled labour. Since WWII, rising labour costs have narrowed the difference in cost and steel has once again been used on some recent bridges. The ability of companies like Harland & Wolff, the Belfast shipbuilders, to fabricate large steel sections also played a part.

FAIRVIEW PARK FOOTBRIDGE, DUBLIN

A somewhat unusual example of a metal footbridge with a truss made up from welded steel tubing. The truss depth has been increased over the central third of the span to counteract the higher bending moments that occur over that portion of the span. Bracing is generally to a Warren arrangement with additional vertical members carried upwards as hoops and providing a degree of cross bracing. The bridge crosses the River Tolka at the East Wall Road entrance to Fairview Park in Dublin.

QEII BRIDGE, BELFAST

For much of the 20th century, concrete construction proved cheaper than steel for short and medium span bridges. More recently, however, various factors have altered this position. When, in 1966, a second river crossing was required to parallel the 1843 Queens Bridge, each to operate unidirectionally, steel was selected as the construction material. The central arch of the QEII Bridge consists of a drop-in section supported by short cantilevers, the weight being balanced by longer cantilevered beams to either side. Like all the River Lagan bridges in Belfast, the foundations are piled. Designer was R. Travers Morgan & Partners, the contractor Charles Brand & Sons Ltd., and Harland & Wolff fabricated the steel.

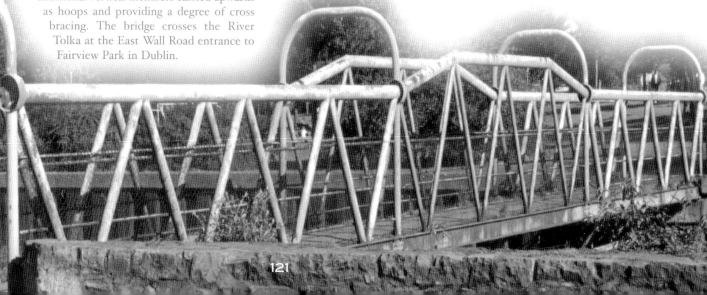

Encasing the steel beams in concrete may obviate the need for periodic painting of structural steel elements. However, few bridges were so constructed. In the 1960s, there was a resurgence of interest in the use of the Preflex version of encased beams and a small number of bridges were built in Northern Ireland using these beams, the first apparently being the new road bridge erected in 1968 at Toome across the Lower Bann in County Derry. ❖

COLERAINE LIFTING RAIL BRIDGE, COUNTY DERRY

The lifting rail bridge across the River Bann at Coleraine in County Derry presents, by contrast, a neater profile than those at Dublin Port, even though the span is longer. Here, the counter-weight is provided by a concrete block supported by wires below the deck, known as the Strauss underhung system. The rolling surface can be seen by the operator's cabin to the right of the ship. The bridge, which is still operational, is approached by fixed plate girder spans, was designed in 1921 by Sir W.H.Armstrong, Whitworth & Co. and was supplied by Dorman Long Steel Company.

SARSFIELD BRIDGE, LIMERICK

The original twin-leaved cast-iron swivel bridge at the east end of Sarsfield Bridge in Limerick was manufactured by Forrester & Co. of Liverpool. This was replaced in 1923 by a steel box single leaf swivel bridge manufactured by the Cleveland Bridge & Engineering Co. of Darlington. The illustration shows the rack and one of the carrying wheels. Usually such bridges were raised slightly to lift the free end off the support before opening commenced. Such bridges tend to jump under live loads and the opening span here has been welded shut.

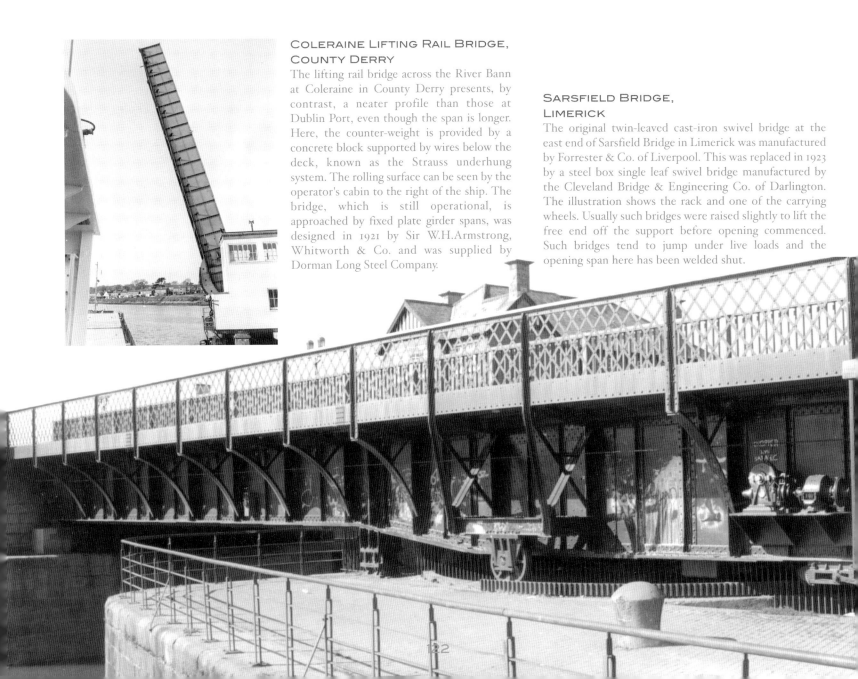

SCHERZER LIFT BRIDGES, DUBLIN

In 1912, the Dublin Port and Docks Board's chief engineer (Sir John Purser Griffith) designed twin-lifting bridges to span the entrance to Spencer Dock at the North Wall Quays. The design was based on the patent of William Scherzer of Chicago, USA and Spencer & Co., of Melksham, Wiltshire manufactured and installed the steel structures. The bridges lifted by rotation along the rack and pinion on the face of the curved girder seen in the illustration. To balance the bridge deck when open, a mass concrete weight was provided at the back of the curved girders. A similar pair of bridges was erected in 1932 over the entrance to the Custom House Docks. The bridges have recently been refurbished.

Chapter Five
Concrete Bridges

Concrete *Bridges*

ridges have been constructed in mass or reinforced concrete since around 1900. Although such bridges tend to be utilitarian in appearance, and often lack any recognisable aesthetic qualities, they nevertheless form an important feature of transport infrastructure. Ireland possesses a range of bridge designs executed in concrete, including examples of both pre-cast and pre-stressed construction.

LITTLE ISLAND INTERCHANGE,
CORK

In 1824, Joseph Aspdin introduced manufactured cement, known as Portland cement. Its appearance was similar to Portland stone, replacing the naturally occurring substance known as Roman cement. At first, there were problems with its manufacture but, once consistent quality Portland cement became available, it was mixed with sand and stone to produce concrete; this material began to be used widely after about 1865.

Concrete has the same disadvantage as cast iron – it is strong in compression but weak in tension. Initially its use was confined to foundation work and as an infilling or 'hearting' to bridge piers and arches. Thus it was used in the Ballydehob Viaduct in West County Cork in 1886 and in Taylorstown Viaduct near Wellingtonbridge in County Wexford in 1906, as well as on Tassagh Viaduct and some bridges on the Armagh & Castleblaney Railway through Keady in County Armagh. Subsequently, mass concrete was used in arch bridges, either built up from concrete blocks replicating stonework or cast solid in one piece. The contractor Sir Robert McAlpine & Sons, in particular, promoted the use of mass concrete for bridges and viaducts, but there are only a few Irish examples.

William Wilkinson realised as early as 1854 that iron bars inserted into the concrete would make it stronger, but little was done initially to develop his ideas due to the difficulty in obtaining bars of a sufficiently consistent strength. It is generally considered that the first practical system of reinforced concrete was that developed in France by Monier (patented in 1867), which used two layers of small diameter round bars. A number of French engineers

CRUIT ISLAND BRIDGE,
COUNTY DONEGAL
A simple utilitarian version of the concrete arch bridge design may be seen at Cruit Island in County Donegal. Here, the deck is carried on solid vertical members down to a solid arch. Designed by Mouchel, the contractor was J & R Thompson of Belfast. The deck extends beyond the 94ft span of the arch in order to utilize the stone abutments of a previous structure. Cruit Island Bridge was built in 1911 for the Congested Districts Board to provide pedestrian access to the island, reputedly for the use of fishermen, although it is now out of use. The deck is unusual in both tapering in plan and rising to the centre.

researched further into reinforced concrete, including Lambot and Coignet, but it was the work of François Hennebique after 1892 that was to lead to the widespread use of reinforced concrete as a construction material.

The granting of a licence by Hennebique to L G Mouchel in 1897 to design works in 'ferro-concrete' led to an explosion of concrete construction in Britain and, somewhat later, in Ireland. Mouchel undertook the design while construction was entrusted to licensed contractors, such as J & R Thompson of Belfast. At this time, concrete often proved to be cheaper than other contemporary forms of construction.

CAMPILE RAIL BRIDGE, COUNTY WEXFORD

Sir Robert McAlpine (known affectionately as 'Concrete Bob') advocated the use of mass concrete for buildings and bridges from around 1876. His firm built this bridge, near Campile in County Wexford on the line from Waterford to Rosslare Harbour, in 1906. The three mass concrete arches on tall concrete piers carry an accommodation crossing and are in good order, as are other works of this period constructed by McAlpine.

ST JOHNS BRIDGE,
KILKENNY

St Johns Bridge, shown here, is an example of the long single span bridges built to the design of Mouchel & Partners. Crossing the River Nore at Kilkenny, with a span of 140ft, it was reputedly the longest reinforced concrete arch road bridge in Britain or Ireland when completed in 1912. It was built by J & R Thompson of Belfast. The arch consists of three ribs, tapering from 2ft 6in. to 2ft in depth, whilst the transverse deck beams are each 2ft deep. When, in 1970, one of the abutments was found to have moved, a new reinforced concrete deck was added and the openings in the arch spandrels were concreted up.

Other designers, seeking to circumvent the various patents then in force, introduced alternative methods of reinforcement, often working on a design-and-build basis. There was considerable debate over whether the use of a large number of small diameter bars was preferable to concentrated reinforcement, such as the Moss rail-type bars used on Hartley Bridge spanning the River Shannon to the north of Carrick-on-Shannon. There was also debate as to whether pre-formed mesh, such as that used by the British Reinforced Concrete Company (BRC) in the bridge spanning the River Slaney at Killurin in County Wexford, or the punched and expanded metal sheets of the Expanded Metal Co., were preferable to individual bars. In some instances, what appears to be a concrete bridge consists of structural

steelwork that has been encased in concrete. This may provide added protection to the steel against rusting. If carried a stage further, such composite steel/concrete structures may be designed so that each material carries part of the applied loads. It is usually not possible to distinguish the type of reinforcement used from the external appearance of the structure, although some designers have incorporated their own distinctive detailing.

SKEW BRIDGE, CAMPILE, COUNTY WEXFORD

Another example of McAlpine's use of concrete on the railway in south County Wexford. Near Campile, the railway crosses the road on a marked skew. Here, the arch is made up of rings of brick, the spiral coursing to the arch barrel and of the face of the rings being clearly seen. The abutments, parapets and spandrel walls are all of concrete, almost certainly in mass form, i.e. without reinforcement. Strong horizontal featuring has been used to break up the plain surfaces.

WADDELLS BRIDGE, COUNTY DERRY

Waddells Bridge represents an unaltered example of Mouchel's pre-war arch bridge design that was used widely throughout Britain and Ireland. The main structural elements are the outer ribs, 2ft 6in. deep by 2ft wide that arch 64ft to the abutments. The deck is carried on transverse beams spanning to longitudinal side beams in the pattern favoured by Mouchel. The load from these side beams is transferred to the arch by square columns at intervals. This arrangement gives a light appearance to the elevation. Although the concrete is somewhat discoloured, the bridge, on a minor road near Draperstown in County Derry, is in good order.

Resistance to shear was provided in ferro-concrete construction by flat bar stirrups, although round bar stirrups later became the norm in reinforced concrete. Kahn bars, with a diamond section having attached fins acting as shear reinforcement, were used in the King's Bridge in Belfast around 1910. Many early bridges did not have the amount of shear reinforcement now considered essential and a number have been strengthened as traffic loadings have increased.

The bond achieved between the reinforcement and the concrete was another matter of some concern. Insufficient bond would allow the bars to pull out under load. Some designers used ribbed bars, such as those used on the Boa Island and Roscor Viaducts in County

Fermanagh by the Indented Bar and Engineering Company, or various forms of twisted bar to improve the bond. Current practice is to continue the bar for a predetermined distance past the point of zero stress or to form a hook on the end of a straight bar.

Early reinforced concrete design almost always suffers from a lack of concrete cover to the reinforcement. In the early days, designers seem to have thought that, once covered in cement, reinforcement would not rust. Cover of as little as 18-25mm was commonplace.

LADY CRAIGAVON BRIDGE, COUNTY FERMANAGH

Designed by Mouchel & Partners, Lady Craigavon Bridge in County Fermanagh was built by contractors A.E.Farr in 1935. This eleven-span structure, together with the thirteen-span Lady Brooke Bridge, provided access from the south bank of Upper Lough Erne to the market town of Lisnaskea, a provision necessitated by the establishment of the Border in 1921. Lady Craigavon Bridge has four higher navigation spans, their cylindrical piers being to Mouchel's patent. The Lady Brooke Bridge has no specific provision for navigation. The bridges consist of longitudinal beams spanning to pairs of solid piers and supporting cross beams extended under the concrete parapet as cantilevers – a design much favoured by Mouchel.

Cover is now more likely to be 37-50mm, perhaps 75mm if under water, and even more for marine environments. Early bridges often show signs of spalling – the breaking off of flakes of concrete due to the rusting of the reinforcement below, which sometimes leaves the reinforcement exposed.

BEAM AND SLAB DECK
A view of the underside of a beam and slab concrete bridge deck. Note the water main bracketed off the parapet in the foreground, a disfiguring feature, typical of many bridges.

KNOCKLYON PEDESTRIAN/CYCLE OVERBRIDGE, DUBLIN

Knocklyon pedestrian/cycle overbridge carries a combined pedestrian/cycleway across the M50 motorway in south Dublin. The slender deck is supported by a cable-stayed system, using spirally wound steel ropes. The distinctive A-frame pylon is constructed in reinforced concrete, whilst the deck combines concrete with a steel box-girder. The bridge is enclosed to protect road users from the potential hazards of vandalism. Design of the bridge was by Ewbank, Preece OhEocha, part of the Mott MacDonald Group, and the contractor was ASCON.

BLANCHARDSTOWN INTERCHANGE, DUBLIN

Near Blanchardstown, in the western suburbs of Dublin, the M50 intersects the N3 Navan road, the railway from Dublin to Sligo, and the Royal Canal. The juxtaposition of these different transportation elements required the construction in the mid-1990s of a number of reinforced concrete over-bridges on this section of the motorway. The N3 merges with a roundabout, which is carried over the motorway on a pair of single span concrete arch bridges. The rail track is carried on a multi-cellular skewed deck supported by a central pier in the motorway median, whilst the canal trough box (aqueduct) was designed as a watertight structure and is also supported by a central pier.

BRÚ NA BÓINNE VISITORS CENTRE FOOTBRIDGE, COUNTY MEATH

This attractive, asymmetric, steel-framed, cable-stayed footbridge provides access across the River Boyne to the Brú na Bóinne Visitors Centre in County Meath. The bridge has an overall length of 68m, the 25m high supporting tower being founded on rock. The bridge, designed for the Office of Public Works by Michael Punch & Partners, was erected in 1996. P Rogers & Sons were the contractors and the consultant architect was Anthony O'Neill.

CROSS HARBOUR LINK BRIDGES, BELFAST

The Lagan Bridge, completed in 1994, extended the M2 motorway across the River Lagan in Belfast and is the only section of the proposed inner motorway box likely to be built - the remainder being a casualty of the 1970s oil crisis. Constructed like the West Link Bridge in Dublin, each segment was cast up against its neighbour to ensure accuracy of jointing, a technique known as match casting. The bridge has spans of 55m, 83m and 55m. Contemporaneously, the adjacent Dargan Bridge was constructed connecting the Larne branch railway to Central Station, at 1425m, the longest railway bridge in Ireland. Designers for the Cross Harbour Links project were Acer Consultants, and the contractors Farrans Construction Ltd. and John Graham (Dromore) Ltd.

ESKE RIVER BRIDGE, COUNTY DONEGAL

The Eske River Bridge on the Donegal Bypass, designed by KML Carl Bro, was the overall winner of the Irish Concrete Society prize in 2000. The designers used the rock foundations to take the thrust of a pair of skewed arches supporting the flat slab deck and thus created a structure that curves in sympathy with the sweep of the river, thus obviating the need for a central pier. The arches taper inwards at their base to give a light open feeling as one passes under the bridge. The contractor was Deane Public Works Ltd.

JAMES JOYCE BRIDGE, DUBLIN

Designed by the internationally renowned Spanish architect and engineer, Santiago Calatravalls, in association with Roughan & O'Donovan of Dublin, this 40m clear span bridge incorporates a pair of striking parabolic arches from which the deck structure is suspended by thirty-two pairs of steel hangers. The arch ribs are inclined outwards and curved in plan, and consist of two steel box sections rising to a height of 8.5m above deck level. The deck is of composite steel/concrete construction and accommodates four lanes of road traffic.

WEXFORD BRIDGE, WEXFORD

A timber bridge over the estuary of the River Slaney at Wexford lasted until 1959, when Ascon Ltd. built a pre-stressed post-tensioned double cantilever bridge to a design of O'Connell & Hartley of Cork. However, a number of these early post-tensioned bridges have given trouble - this example having problems at the joints between the cantilevered arms. Consequently, in 1997, the pre-stressed concrete cantilevers were removed and a lighter continuous steel girder structure with a composite concrete deck slab was erected on the existing piers and abutments. The bridge, designed by J.B.Barry & Partners, and again built by Ascon, has seven spans, giving a total length of 383m. Wexford Bridge received a Construction Excellence award in 1998.

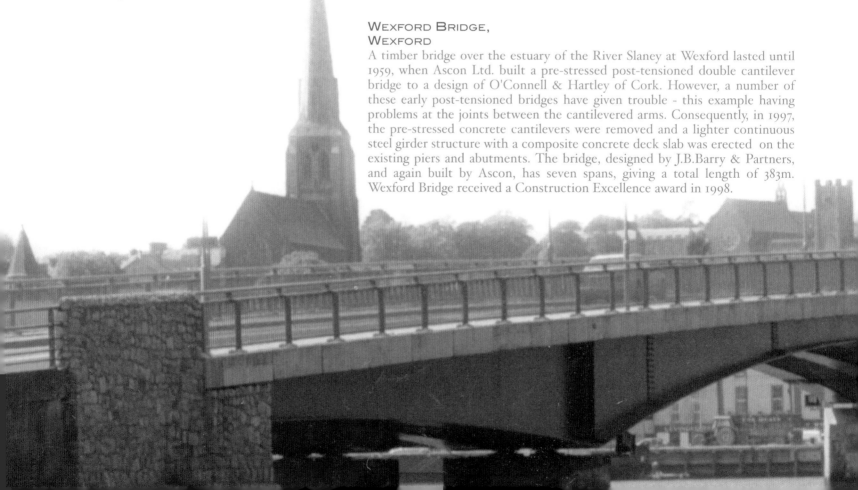

AGHALANE BRIDGE, COUNTY CAVAN/FERMANAGH BORDER

The bridge at Aghalane, on the County Cavan/Fermanagh border, is a stone-faced concrete structure. It crosses the Woodford River, part of the Shannon-Erne Waterway, and the intention of the design is to blend in with the older structures on the waterway. The consultant, W D R & R T Taggart, designed special pre-cast concrete sections for use on the bridge, these being manufactured by Macrete. The contractor was Deane Public Works Ltd.

ST PATRICK'S FOOTBRIDGE, COUNTY TYRONE

St Patrick's footbridge, over the Omagh through-pass in County Tyrone, is situated between two large schools to the west of the town and is of an unusual arrangement. The basic support is in the form of a steel arch. The deck, however, is elevated such that it is supported near to its ends directly off the arch, whilst the central section is suspended using three hangers. The structure is of welded steel hollow sections, supplied in 1991 by IES Steel Structures Ltd to a design prepared by the Omagh Division of the DoE for NI Roads Service. The span is around 21m.

ECOS MILLENIUM CENTRE BRIDGE, COUNTY ANTRIM

This elegant steel structure, completed in 2000, carries the cycle and pedestrian way to the Ecos Millenium Centre in Ballymena. It is curved in plan to a constant 140m radius, and rises to a high point over the central pier. Designed by W D R & R T Taggart, and built by GEDA Construction of Dungannon. The ten spans, making up the 150ft long structure over the River Braid and its flood plain, form one continuous beam, fixed at the central support.

SARSFIELD ROAD BRIDGE, CORK

This seven-span glued, segmental, match-cast, post-tensioned bridge spanning the Sarsfield Road roundabout on the Southern Ring Road in Cork was designed by Fehily Timoney & Associates and built by HMC Construction in 1995. With an overall length of 227m, and a central span of 50.5m, it laid claim to have been the world's second longest continuous post-tensioned pedestrian/cycle bridge at the time of its construction. The flowing soffit of the bridge is particularly attractive.

MACKEN STREET BRIDGE, DUBLIN

A computer-generated impression of the 120m long cable-stayed opening bridge, designed by Santiago Calatrava Valls, S.A., in association with Roughan & O'Donovan, and selected for the Guild Street – Macken Street crossing of the River Liffey downstream of the city centre. The single supporting pylon, to be located about 28m from the face of the south quays, has a curved profile leaning northwards and will rise to a height of approximately 48m. Both the main span and the back span are to be constructed as steel box girders, with the end of the back span filled with concrete in order to provide the required counterweight to the longer main span. The uneven lengths of the two spans will have equal weights enabling the bridge to be balanced about the pylon base so that it can be swung open to accommodate river navigation.

MILLENNIUM BRIDGE, DUBLIN

Completed in December 1999, the Millennium Bridge crosses the River Liffey in Dublin with a single shallow rise span of 41m. Design of this footbridge was won in open competition, against 152 other entries, by the architectural practice of Howley Harrington and structural engineers Price and Myers. The bridge structure is an asymmetrical parabolic arch truss, the ends being supported off stone-clad abutments. It is constructed from steel and aluminium, giving light and clean proportions. The bridge was awarded the Royal Institute of Architects of Ireland Regional Prize in 2000. The main contractor was ASCON, fabrication of the structure being by Thomas Thompson of Carlow.

KILMACANOGUE FOOTBRIDGE, COUNTY WICKLOW

This stressed ribbon footbridge spans 48m across the N11 dual carriageway at Kilmacanogue in County Wicklow. The 2.8m long 300mm thick trough-section concrete deck units were cast on site, lifted up, and then strapped on to the six pre-tensioned bearing cables or tendons. Each unit was then winched into place along the bearing cables, without any interruption to traffic. When all units were placed, the concrete deck was completed and the whole post-tensioned. Design was by Roughan & Donovan and the contractor was Clonmel Enterprises.

NEW BOYNE BRIDGE, COUNTY LOUTH

Designed by Roughan & O'Donovan, this cable-stayed bridge, with a main span of 170m, was built to carry the M1 across an environmentally sensitive stretch of the Boyne River two kilometres to the west of Drogheda. The single concrete pylon obviates the need for any temporary or permanent supports in the river. The 34.5m wide steel composite deck caters for three lanes of traffic in each direction. The entire under-croft of the deck is housed within a high-strength plastic enclosure, providing a low corrosion atmosphere around the unpainted steel, yet allowing full access for inspection.

CASTLE BRIDGE,
COUNTY FERMANAGH

Increasing traffic in the town centre of Enniskillen in County Fermanagh led to the construction of a through-pass, with a parallel crossing upstream of West Bridge. Castle Bridge, originally proposed in 1973 as a steel box structure, was completed in 1982 in reinforced concrete. The design, prepared by the NII Roads Service, has beams forming 'splay-legged portal frames', as the illustration clearly shows. The main span is 48m and the length 64m. The parapet was specially designed to improve driver visibility, as the bridge ends at a junction with the Sligo road. The contractor was Farrans Ltd. of Belfast.

NEW SHAW'S BRIDGE,
COUNTY ANTRIM/DOWN BORDER

Shaws Bridge on the County Antrim/Down border occupied a long-established crossing point on the River Lagan. The stone structure was built in 1709, but three arches were rebuilt as two in 1740. This bridge continued to carry modern traffic, although two buses could not pass on it. The development of a nearby housing estate necessitated the construction of a replacement structure alongside. New Shaw's Bridge, opened in 1976, is a single span post-tensioned arch. The abutments, which are cross-tied below water level, are splayed back to afford a clear view of the stone bridge behind. The zigzag pathway between the two bridges provides wheelchair access to the towpath.

Concrete was originally hand mixed and tamped into temporary falsework (or formwork), needed to support the wet concrete until it had hardened and gained its strength. Greenisland Viaduct in County Antrim, completed in 1932, was reportedly the first major structure to make widespread use of mechanical vibration, either applied externally to the formwork or directly to the wet concrete using vibrating pokers. The application of vibration when placing concrete is now universal. Wet concrete exerts a considerable pressure on the supporting formwork that has to be resisted by temporary scaffolding around the proposed structure. To

Gweebarra Bridge, County Donegal

The Gweebarra road bridge in County Donegal, which might more correctly be referred to as a road viaduct, is an impressive structure of nine 60ft main spans, with half spans of just over 28ft at either end. The deck, which consists of an 18ft wide roadway with two 4ft 6in. wide footpaths, is supported on sets of four 4ft deep longitudinal beams with a shallow arch profile. These are carried on 5ft 6in. by 3ft wide transverse beams, which in turn are supported on 6ft diameter piers. The concrete pierced balustrades act successfully as a foil to the rather massive nature of the structure. The bridge was completed in 1953 by the Irish Engineering & Harbour Construction Company.

Exposed reinforcement, County Antrim

Detail showing reinforcement exposed due to spalling of the concrete as a result of a low concrete cover. The structure, dated 1914 on the parapet in the style of bridges designed by the LMS NCC Railway, was built to carry the narrow 3ft gauge railway to the British Aluminium plant at Larne harbour over the main line. The 3ft gauge railways in County Antrim ceased to operate many years ago and the bridge now stands abandoned.

reduce the overall size of this scaffolding, the concrete is often placed in small amounts, called lifts or pours that are then left to harden before the next amount is placed. This can result in joint lines (sometimes disguised as features) visible at the surface or, unfortunately, adjacent sections of concrete of a slightly different colour.

Early cements were coarsely ground powders whilst modern cements tend to be more finely ground. The strength of early concrete increased relatively slowly and then continued to increase for some considerable time. Recent tests undertaken on concrete samples taken from bridges of the LMS NCC Railway from the 1930s failed at loads of between three and four times the design load. Modern cements gain strength more quickly, allowing for the earlier removal of the formwork, but then do not continue over time to gain strength to the same degree.

MULLAN COT BRIDGE, COUNTY TYRONE/DERRY BORDER

Mullan Cot Bridge, on the County Tyrone/Derry border, is a 193ft 3in. long footbridge. This slender structure was constructed in 1924-5 to provide access across the Ballinderry River to the chapel at Killymuck. Reportedly funded by Tyrone and Derry County Councils, responsibility for footpaths away from roads appears not to have passed to the NI Roads Service and the bridge is not currently being maintained. Long edge beams are carried on four pairs of supporting legs, three simply cross-braced and one completed solid. Designed by Mouchel & Partners, the approved Hennibique contractor, Robert Calhoun Ltd, was employed for its construction.

**MARMION BRIDGE,
EDERMINE,
COUNTY WEXFORD**

Mention is made elsewhere of the slender supports used for Hartley Bridge, but the single carriageway road bridge spanning the River Slaney at Edermine in County Wexford has even simpler supports. These consist of a capping/deck beam supported on two raked columns or piles, designed to withstand flood conditions. These slender supports may be compared with the robust piers seen on such bridges as that at Mountgarret. Marmion Bridge was erected by Irishenco in 1974-5 to replace an 1898 bridge of timber and metal. The bridge was named after Don Columba Marmion, the Abbot of the Benedictine monks of Maredsous in Belgium who took refuge from WWI in nearby Edermine House.

Strength and compaction both play a part in determining the durability of concrete. Fortunately, Ireland does not suffer from the levels of atmospheric pollution found in some countries, but problems have been encountered with the penetration of salt used for road de-icing, especially on motorway bridges, leading to rusting of the reinforcement.

Pre-casting is the term used when sections or elements of a structure are cast away from the site and brought to the site for erection. Pre-casting allows work to be undertaken under much more even and controllable conditions. An obvious first form of pre-casting was the manufacture of concrete blocks, sometimes referred to as cast-stone. These may be employed in the same way as stone or brick in arch bridges. There are, however, surprisingly few examples in Ireland of this option. Bridges having pre-cast deck beams or pre-cast columns

RICE BRIDGE, COUNTY WATERFORD

In 1794, an American carpenter, by the name of Lemuel Cox, erected an 832ft long timber trestle bridge across the River Suir at Waterford. This bridge, known affectionately as "Old Timber Toes", was replaced in 1910 by a Mouchel designed ferro-concrete structure. This, in turn, was replaced with the present bridge, a twin-leaf opening bridge of the bascule type with pre-stressed concrete approach spans. Rice Bridge, opened to traffic in 1986, was designed by Rendel, Palmer & Tritton, and constructed by Irishenco.

LETTER BRIDGE, COUNTY DONEGAL

Letter Bridge, near Pettigo in County Donegal, is one of the structures repaired recently following earlier cratering. The 16m span of the new bridge consists of pre-cast Y-beams and the photograph shows these being lifted into place by the contractor, Deane Public Works Ltd. of Killadeas. Design of the bridge was undertaken by the Western Division of the NI Roads Service. (Photo: Deane Public Works)

RIVER FAUGHAN BRIDGE, COUNTY DERRY

The LMS NCC Railway designed and used pre-cast concrete elements innovatively for bridge construction (both in over- and under-bridges) from 1912. This work culminated in the multi-span Kellswater Bridge (1935) and the viaducts at the Rivers Faughan and Roe (1937-39), all of which replaced light girder structures. The River Faughan Bridge in County Derry has eight flat spans. The deck consists of four deep T-beams (two per running rail) and outer parapet beams with pronounced recessed feature panels. The stone end abutments were reused but the river piers were rebuilt in concrete. The bridge was designed at the railway company's York Road drawing office in Belfast and built by direct labour.

MOUNT NORRIS BRIDGE, COUNTY ARMAGH

The old turnpike road between Newry and Armagh crossed the River Cusher near Mount Norris in County Armagh. At this point, an earlier bridge was replaced with one using 33ft long pre-stressed concrete beams, pre-cast by Dow-Mac at Warrenpoint. The parapet was completed as a rather crude solid slab and has since been repaired. Although considered as 'trail-blazing' when built, such structures are now commonplace throughout Ireland.

or balustrades are more commonplace. One of the first bridges to employ large pre-cast elements was the footbridge to the Mizen Head lighthouse in West Cork, erected in 1909. Here, the arch was made up from U-shaped trough sections, which, once in place, were filled with concrete. Examples of the use of big segments, generally three in number, to make up a beam may be seen on some of the Northern Ireland motorway bridges.

As concrete is weak in tension, the carrying load on a beam may be increased if it is first put into compression. This is the underlying principle of pre-stressing, with the first practical experiments being undertaken on the European mainland in the 1930s. Wires, usually called

tendons, are placed and then stretched before being anchored against the end of the beam. Release of the stressing-jack then introduces compression in the beam. Pre-stressed beams may be either pre-tensioned or post-tensioned. Pre-tensioning is useful for small beams, and for items such as fence posts or guardrails, and was the system first used. The wires are stretched on a frame in the casting yard and the beams are cast around them. A continuous bond thus exists between the concrete and the tendon. First used in 1952 in a road bridge replacement over the main rail line near Sallins in County Kildare, and, shortly thereafter in a bridge at Mount Norris in County Armagh, pre-tensioned beams are now widely encountered.

The alternative method, and that needed for large beams, is to cast the beam first, leaving ducts for the tendons. These are then threaded in and stressed after the beam has attained its design strength. There is now no continuous bond with the concrete. At first, attempts were

MALAHIDE
RAIL VIADUCT,
COUNTY DUBLIN

The twelve-span 577ft long rail viaduct spanning the mouth of the estuary north of Malahide station on the Dublin/Belfast main line has been rebuilt twice since its original construction in timber in 1844. Replaced with wrought-iron latticed girders in 1860 and strengthened in 1932, the viaduct was rebuilt between 1966 and 1968 using pre-stressed pre-cast concrete units, each varying in weight from 20 to 38tons. When completed, Malahide Viaduct had the largest pre-cast superstructure in Ireland.

CONCRETE RAIL OVERBRIDGE,
COUNTY KILDARE

The first pre-stressed concrete bridge to be completed in Ireland, was erected in 1952 west of Naas in County Kildare over the Dublin-Cork main railway line, to replace a cast-iron structure whose strength was deemed inadequate for modern road traffic. Fifteen 37ft 6in. long concrete beams, pre-stressed using the Lee McCall system, were craned into position side by side to form the bridge. A reinforced concrete slab was laid in situ to form the deck. The bridge was designed by the staff of the Civil Engineering Department of Córas Iompair Éireann, who carried out the replacement in twenty-four hours without any interruption to rail traffic.

(Iarnród Éireann)

ANNESLEY BRIDGE, DUBLIN

In 1925, a contract was awarded to Orr, Watt & Co. of Motherwell for the rebuilding of Annesley Bridge over the River Tolka in Dublin to a design of M A Moynihan, which used a mixture of steel and concrete. The concrete deck was cast on steel troughing carried on 2 ft deep longitudinal I-beams at a 5ft spacing. On the advice of Sir John Purser-Griffith, it was proposed to drive 50ft long piles to support the widening. In the event, it proved necessary to pile the entire foundations and Robert McAlpine was contracted to install Wolfscholtz pressure-grouted piles. These foundation difficulties delayed the opening of the three-span structure until 1928.

TAYLORSTOWN RAILWAY VIADUCT, COUNTY WEXFORD

Detail of the brick face of the Taylorstown railway viaduct in County Wexford showing staining caused by effervescence leaching out from the mass concrete hearting. The red brick contrasts sharply with the white runs of leachate.

made to fill the duct with cement grout but the effectiveness of this procedure is debatable. The viaduct near Dee Street on the Sydenham Bypass in Belfast was built in 1959, but concerns over water ingress and possible rusting of the tendons led to its demolition in 1998. Large span modern bridges are now frequently made up of a number of segments strung together in the manner of pearls on a necklace. The joints between each segment are glued using special epoxy resins, the beams subsequently being post-tensioned.

Mention has been made of the early use of mass concrete (no steel reinforcement) in foundations. After 1900, Mouchel developed a system for the design and use of pre-cast reinforced concrete piles, which could be driven into the ground to provide support for bridge piers. An outer cylinder was used as a guide for the pile group, usually three per cylinder, and this was later built up in concrete to form a cylindrical pier. A number of

examples of the use of this technique may be seen in Ireland.

Without doubt, the major disadvantage of concrete for bridgework lies in its appearance. In cases in the past, little attempt was made to add any features to the concrete surface – features only added to the difficulties in casting and thus increased the overall cost of the bridge. The commonest feature, especially on early bridges, was the casting of panels, usually

CARRY BRIDGE, COUNTY FERMANAGH

Although Carry Bridge in County Fermanagh continues the same general design arrangement as that of certain other 1930s bridges, it was built later (1956). The bridge was designed by the NI Ministry of Finance (Works Department) as part of a drainage scheme for Lough Erne. The previous bridge on the site, rebuilt in 1843 to facilitate navigation, had a stone arch of unusual horseshoe shape either side of a lattice girder span. The main design feature of the present bridge is the slab deck carried on three-column portal frames to the solid arch. The span is 140 ft and the overall width 24 ft. The contractor was Farrans Ltd. of Belfast.

GRIFFITH PARK FOOTBRIDGE, DUBLIN

Designed by the engineering staff of Dublin Corporation, this footbridge in Griffith Park in Dublin is an example of a small composite structure. The 3ft 6in. wide end supports and 4ft wide central support are formed in mass concrete. These carry a steel I-beam under each parapet. Smaller cross I-beams (two in each of the two 18ft spans) support the 8ft 9in wide concrete deck, reinforced with mesh. Mesh reinforcement is also used in the parapet. The nature of this reinforcement means that the parapet has to be solid, giving the bridge an unduly heavy appearance.

slightly recessed, into the solid parapets. In a few cases, like Carry Bridge at Lough Erne in County Fermanagh (1956), concrete pieced balustrades, often pre-cast, have been used with better effect than solid parapets. Perhaps surprisingly, solid parapets are not always the strongest. Too often, there are only a few dowelling bars (short pieces of reinforcement) connecting the parapet to the bridge deck. Thus the strengthening of concrete bridges often entails the replacement of the parapets, sometimes in metal, which does not always add to the appearance of the bridge. Other techniques used to improve the appearance of bridges are the casting of vertical or horizontal flutes or raised bands, or the bush hammering of the formed surface to expose the aggregate, thus making the surface resemble pebbledash.

Most concrete bridges have a flat-deck profile, either with pre-cast beams or cast in situ slabs, with or without attached beams. The flat profile is occasionally relieved by incorporating a drop-down to the support. Arch bridges tend to look more pleasing and some good examples exist with open spandrels to the arch. In the 1930s, a number of bridges with a bowstring profile were built, that at Kenmare in County Kerry being typical. Given the

DESIGNER CONCRETE,
COUNTY ANTRIM
The face of a bridge built in 1927 showing an early attempt at concrete featuring. Strong horizontal lines, which also disguise the joints, are offset by exposed white aggregate on the face of the parapet. The work here extended an earlier stone culvert carrying a footpath and was undertaken as part of the doubling of the rail line from Carrickfergus and Whitehead in County Antrim.

**ULSTER FOLK & TRANSPORT MUSEUM BRIDGE,
CULTRA, COUNTY DOWN**

Trustees installed the Ulster Folk & Transport Museum entrance bridge at
Cultra in County Down in 1970 to remove the need for traffic to turn across
the busy Belfast to Bangor road. The structure with its unusually shaped
arch received a judges' mention in the 1971 Concrete Society awards. Six
profiled Preflex beams span 63ft, and pre-cast soffit panels form a working
platform clear of the main road. The north box abutment is carried on 25ft
long 24in. diameter piles to the underlying rock. Design was by J T A
McAuley & Partners and the contractor was A J Clancy Ltd.

problem of lack of tensile strength, this type of bridge built in concrete has much thicker
hangers than would be required if using steel. Large motorway interchanges, which
incorporate several individual concrete bridges, appeared in Ireland with the opening of the
first section of the M1 south of Belfast in 1962. The bridges on the early sections are of solid
appearance with solid slab piers. As confidence in the use of concrete has grown amongst
designers, the appearance of concrete bridges has become lighter with continuous beams and
solid piers being replaced by open V-sections or rows of columns. Despite such changes,

concrete still continues to exhibit a broadly utilitarian appearance.

A further problem with concrete is that the surface tends to weather badly. Cracks and joints allow water to leach out leaving lines and runs of white effervescence on the surface. Moss and lichens can also grow on the surface and, while these can give a masonry arch a pleasing aged appearance, on concrete the effect tends to be one of scruffy neglect. The three bridges built north of Belfast in advance of the motorway (later the M2) were backfilled until

PIER DETAILING, BRAY, COUNTY WICKLOW.

An example of imaginative treatment of reinforced concrete piers on a recently completed skewed interchange bridge on the N11 near Bray in County Wicklow.

DECK SECTIONS

Cross-sections of concrete bridge decks showing, from top, simple slab, beam and slab, pre-cast T-beams and pre-cast I-beams.

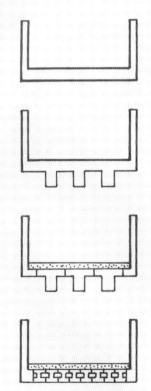

BRIDGE FACE TREATMENT
Modern treatment of a bridge face using heavily ribbed concrete surfaces. This, however, has not deterred the graffiti writers from practising their art form!

ABUTMENT DETAILING, DUBLIN
An example of a modern treatment of bridge abutments, here on one of the M50/N2 interchange bridges on the Dublin ring motorway.

the actual road construction commenced and, as a result, they have been soil-stained ever since, Hightown being an example. Attempts have been made to disguise this with concrete paint but, like all paintwork, one needs to reapply it from time to time to keep up a good appearance. Unfortunately, flat concrete surfaces form an irresistible attraction to the slogan writers and the spray-can artists, detracting further from such a bridge's appearance.

Balanced segmental construction has been used for large motorway bridges. This construction technique involves sections of cast concrete being erected alternately to either side of a support, such that the out-of-balance force on the support is never more that that due to one segment. Match casting allows for more efficient jointing between the segments. During match casting a segment is formed in the casting yard and allowed to harden. Its neighbour is then cast against the end, thus ensuring a perfect fit. The first section is next taken and placed in the bridge, the second segment is moved across and its neighbour is cast

MOUNTGARRET BRIDGE,
COUNTY KILKENNY/WEXFORD BORDER

By 1930, reinforced concrete construction had tended to become lighter, although some designers preferred to use solid circular piers replicating the cast-iron columns of earlier railway bridge works – Mountgarret Bridge on the County Kilkenny/Wexford border is a typical example. Four fixed concrete spans are each of 29ft 6in. The lifting span over the River Barrow is of the Scherzer rolling type, the extra weight being accommodated on a 23ft 6in. platform. The solid cylindrical piers appear to be of the patented Mouchel type. The contractor was John Hearne & Co. whilst John Butler & Co. of Leeds supplied the steel opening span.

V-COLUMN SUPPORTS
Example of a row of open V-column supports, used here on a typical modern reinforced concrete flyover bridge.

up against it. This continues until one half of the structure has reached a little short of mid-span. When the corresponding half has been erected from the adjacent support, the two are formed into one continuous span by means of an in situ concrete 'stitch'.

Although concrete as a construction material is not without its problems, its cost effectiveness and ability to span large gaps will ensure that it continues to be used for many bridge structures in the foreseeable future. ❖

Killurin Bridge,
County Wexford

Killurin Bridge in County Wexford was built in 1915 by the British Reinforced Concrete Engineering Co., working with consultants Delap & Waller (Dublin) and Wexford County Council. The reinforcement is BRC fabric. Crossing the River Slaney at a point known as "The Deeps", navigation is accommodated by a 40ft steel lifting span supplied by Cleveland Engineering Co. There are five spans to either side, generally of 30ft. The width between parapets, unusually formed of concrete Xs, is 18ft 4in. The concrete work exhibits the typical plain solid appearance of bridges of the period.

CHAPTER SIX

RECENT DEVELOPMENTS

Recent Developments

uring the past ten to fifteen years, there has been a significant development of Ireland's infrastructure, much of it resulting from an upsurge in economic activity and the provision of European Union and state funding. New road building, road improvements and the upgrading of the rail infrastructure have resulted in the rehabilitation or replacement of

many bridges on existing routes and the erection of numbers of new bridges on, under or over motorways, bypasses and other parts of the improved transportation infrastructure. In particular, the upgrading of that section of Euroroute I in Ireland linking the ports of Larne in County Antrim with Rosslare Europort in County Wexford by way of Belfast and Dublin, has contributed to a large increase in bridge construction activity. The provision of new river crossings has resulted in a variety of design solutions and construction techniques being used in Ireland, many for the first time.

POINT OF WHITECOAT FOOTBRIDGE, COUNTY ARMAGH

This unusual A-frame tubular steel footbridge at Point of Whitecoat near Portadown in County Armagh was designed to provide a visible feature in an otherwise flat area. It was provided by Craigavon Borough Council to carry the Ulster Way (a long distance footpath which circumscribes Ulster) across the River Cusher. The 25m span was fabricated off-site and installed during one day in 1990. The contractor was Charles Brand Ltd., design having been undertaken by Dr Doran & Partners.

Bypasses have been provided to remove heavy through-traffic from congested town centres and road alignments improved by the removal of sharp bends, often the result of the reluctance of early bridge builders to construct bridges on a skew. Significant investment has continued to be made in strengthening existing bridges to accommodate the heavier axle loads of commercial traffic now permitted by the European Commission.

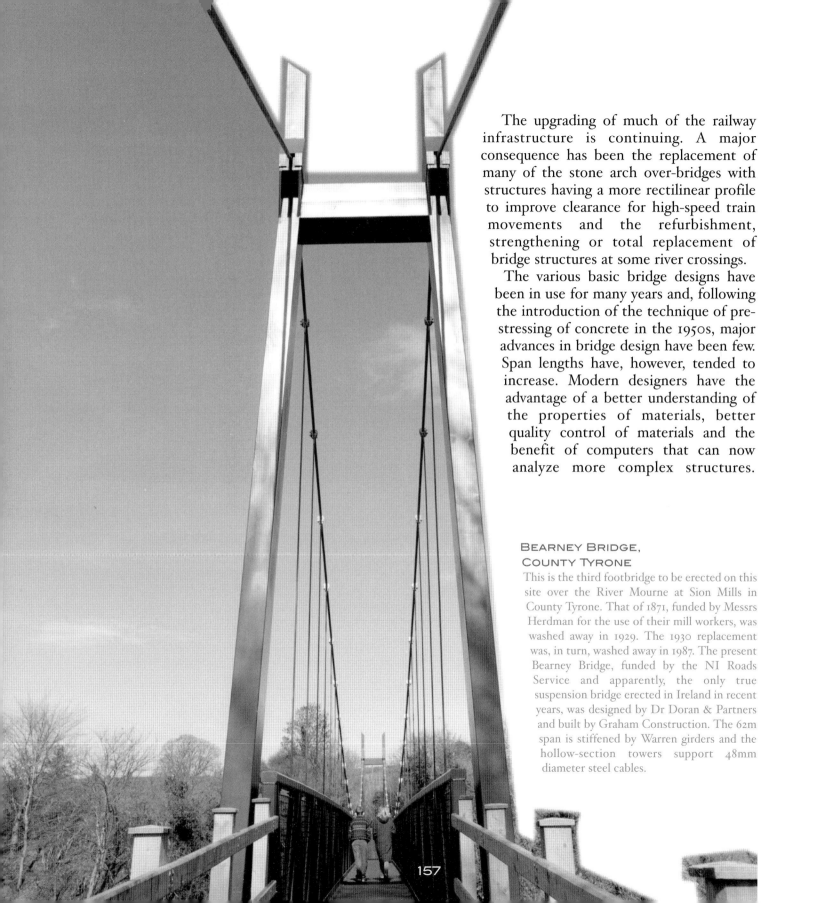

The upgrading of much of the railway infrastructure is continuing. A major consequence has been the replacement of many of the stone arch over-bridges with structures having a more rectilinear profile to improve clearance for high-speed train movements and the refurbishment, strengthening or total replacement of bridge structures at some river crossings.

The various basic bridge designs have been in use for many years and, following the introduction of the technique of pre-stressing of concrete in the 1950s, major advances in bridge design have been few. Span lengths have, however, tended to increase. Modern designers have the advantage of a better understanding of the properties of materials, better quality control of materials and the benefit of computers that can now analyze more complex structures.

BEARNEY BRIDGE, COUNTY TYRONE

This is the third footbridge to be erected on this site over the River Mourne at Sion Mills in County Tyrone. That of 1871, funded by Messrs Herdman for the use of their mill workers, was washed away in 1929. The 1930 replacement was, in turn, washed away in 1987. The present Bearney Bridge, funded by the NI Roads Service and apparently, the only true suspension bridge erected in Ireland in recent years, was designed by Dr Doran & Partners and built by Graham Construction. The 62m span is stiffened by Warren girders and the hollow-section towers support 48mm diameter steel cables.

WEST LINK TOLL BRIDGE, DUBLIN

Motorway construction in the Republic of Ireland commenced much later than in Northern Ireland. However, European Union grants have led to substantial improvements in road infrastructure in the Republic. The West Link Toll Bridge, opened in 1990, carries the Dublin Ring motorway (M50) over the River Liffey, with five spans between 66m and 90m. The deck structure is comprised of pre-cast concrete segments forming box girders, placed either side of the piers such that the out-of-balance load across each pier, during construction, never exceeded one segment, a technique known as segmental balanced cantilever construction. The segments were then post-tensioned. Designers were Ove Arup & Partners, and the contractors a consortium of Irishenco and Dycherhoff & Widman AG. A similar bridge, currently under construction alongside, will ease conjestion at the toll booths. (*The Engineers Journal*, June, 1990)

Recent trends in bridge construction have been towards a greater use of pre-cast elements. These can be manufactured more accurately with better quality control off-site. Recent bridge projects have generally favoured segmental concrete construction (such as the West Link Toll Bridge in Dublin and the Cross Harbour Bridges in Belfast), but there have also been some examples built in steel (for example the Foyle and Wexford Bridges)

Modern construction has now to be cost effective and this may result in bridges being built to a standard pattern with few frills. However, this low cost requirement need not equate to a reduction in aesthetic quality. Design proposals in 1981 for a new road crossing of the River Shannon north of Athlone on the County Westmeath/Roscommon border, for example, included design considerations for reinforced concrete box girder bridges with 3, 5, 7 and 11 spans. Of the four designs, the cheapest, and the one finally selected, also turned out to be the most elegant and appropriate for the location. However, when a cable-stayed bridge was proposed for the Coleraine Bypass in County Londonderry, it proved cheaper to use steel beams continuous over the five spans. This bridge, with a total length of 232 m, and one of the longest bridges in Ulster, was opened in 1975. Modern steel bridges have smooth faces, which allows for easier painting, but they lack the fine ornamental detailing of early cast-iron examples.

Research into the efficient design of pre-cast concrete beams has resulted in the design of a range of standard types and their more frequent use. For example, a system of pre-cast arch sections, 2.5m wide, for carrying roads over railways (or canals) on a marked skew, has been developed.

However, an awareness of the impact on the visual environment of bridges is growing and recent constructions have seen a marked improvement in bridge aesthetics. For example, considerable improvement in the appearance of concrete work can result from the use of pre-cast facing panels or special formwork to mould the concrete. Improvements have come partly from more contracts being awarded on a design-and-build basis in open competition. The requirement of the European Commission, that contracts above a certain size must be advertised throughout the Community, has increased the range of companies tendering for such competitions. Increasingly, such works are being undertaken on a total package basis, with the project being carried out from conception to completion by the competition winner (often a consortium of companies). On the one hand, this process may serve to drive down the cost, on the other, it may provide an impetus for more innovative design, as has been evidenced by some of recent bridge designs, such as the Millennium and James Joyce bridges, and the proposed Guild Street-Macken Street bridge over the River Liffey in Dublin.

TULLAMORE FOOTBRIDGE, COUNTY OFFALY

Light steel sections were used to form N-trusses in this footbridge spanning the Grand Canal in Tullamore in County Offaly. The bridge was designed with an arched profile so as to provide adequate headroom for canal traffic.

Taney Bridge carries Line B of the LUAS light-rail transit system across a very busy intersection in south Dublin. The designers, Roughan & O'Donovan were constrained to providing a structure with no piers located within the junction and with a restricted number of weekend road closures for the construction phase. The solution adopted was an asymmetrical cable-stayed bridge with a total length of 162m. The 108.5m main span of the slim, elegantly curved, concrete deck was constructed using match-cast units glued and stressed together, whilst the remaining spans were cast in situ. The deck is supported from a 45m high cast-concrete pylon by thirteen pairs of steel cables.

The concept of a cable–stayed bridge is not new, but a recent upsurge in their use has resulted mainly from the fact that they offer the opportunity of crossing large obstacles with elegance and economy. However, this type of design is equally suitable for small and medium-span structures, which tend to be far more numerous. The reasons that can lead to the choice of a cable-stayed solution are many, but one of the principal advantages is the clearance available below the deck; the difference in the layouts of the cable-stays is one of the fundamental and distinguishing elements. The use of composite steel/concrete decks allows for a considerable reduction in the dead weight of such structures and in a simplification of their method of erection.

Although bridges do not represent the bulk of the expenditure on new road works, they do have a high visual impact on the public who use these transportation facilities. Motorway over-bridges are frequently of a standard design, but attempts are now usually made to vary the detailing of piers and abutments to good effect, or to use the arch form to produce a more aesthetically pleasing structure, provided that a suitable foundation is available. Structural engineers and architects therefore put considerable effort into producing bridge designs that are both structurally sound and visually acceptable. Each bridge should have its own individuality, it should be suitable for its location and should, where possible, enhance rather than detract from the landscape of its setting. On completion, every new bridge immediately becomes part of our built environment and will in time come to be regarded as an integral part of our built heritage. ❖

KILLARNEY ROAD INTERCHANGE,
BRAY, COUNTY WICKLOW

This interchange on the N11 Dublin to Wexford dual-carriageway provides access to the Southern Cross bypass of Bray, to the town itself and to Enniskerry in County Wicklow. The imaginative detailing of the reinforced concrete median piers has recently been repeated on the route south beyond Kilmacanogue.

Index

Index

Jerretts Pass Bridge, County Down

This bridge over the Newry Canal at Jerretts Pass in County Down, with its rather unusual parapet profile rising to a point and with end roundels, has been attributed to the canal engineer John Brownrigg (ca 1808).

Glossary

Glossary *of Technical Terms*

Abutment the resistance offered to the horizontal thrust of an arch or, more generally, the body which provides the resistance, e.g. at the ends of a bridge

Aedicule a niche flanked by columns to form a recess, sometimes to accommodate a statue

Anchorage the means of restraining or anchoring the ends of the suspended cable(s) of a suspension bridge

Arch a structural element with a curved soffit capable of spanning a horizontal gap and of carrying its own weight and other loads wholly or largely by internal compression

Arch Ring the assembly of voissoirs in a masonry arch between the extrados and the intrados (also arch rib)

Archivolt a projecting moulding that follows the curve of a masonry arch on top of the extrados

Ashlar masonry comprising stones that have been carefully hewn and worked

Balustrade a railing supported by a series of short ornamental pillars or balusters

Beam a usually straight structural member capable of spanning a horizontal gap and supporting loads and transferring them to its supports by its resistance to bending

ARCH RINGS CONSIST OF VOUSSOIRS WITH A KEYSTONE AT THE TOP

Bearing the support of a beam or girder or the length (or area) of the beam or girder that rests on its supports

Bending Moment an angular rotation, being the product of a transverse force and the perpendicular distance to the point at which the moment acts

Bowstring Girder a latticed girder the longitudinal profile, of which has a top flange or chord that is arched or bowed

Box Girder a hollow girder having a square, rectangular or trapezoidal cross-section

BRC Fabric a continuous wire mesh of drawn wires laid in concrete along the lines where the tension is greatest

Buckled Plate a cast- or wrought-iron square or rectangular plate having a convex form to resist downward loads

Cable-stayed a form of suspension bridge in which the deck is supported by a series of cables radiating ftom the towers

Caisson watertight, open-topped box within which the foundations of piers may be constructed

Cantilever a structural member fixed at one end and frequently unsupported along its length, although it may be propped by an intermediate support

Cast-Iron iron that is poured molten into moulds to form castings of the required shape

Cement a powdery substance made by calcining lime and clay, mixed with water to form mortar or used in concrete to bind the aggregate

Centring the temporary structure used to support an arch during its erection

Chord the top or bottom, generally horizontal, part of a metal, timber, or concrete girder

CABLE -STAYED VERSUS SUSPENSION

Clapper Bridge a bridge across a shallow river bed comprising a series of low stone piers spanned by stone slabs

Column a vertical structural member carrying a downward load in compression

Compression a force that tends to shorten a structural member; the opposite of tension

Concrete a composition of gravel, sand, cement and water

Continuous Beam a beam of several spans in the same straight line joined together in such a way that a known load on one span will produce an effect on the others

Corne de Vache French term for tapered chamfering of the edges of arches

Cornice a horizontal moulded projection crowning a building or structure

Crown the highest point of an arch, about the keystone abutment

Cutwater the end of a bridge pier protruding beyond the face of the spandrel and shaped in order to divide the stream of water and deflect floating objects away from the bridge

Dead Load a load of constant magnitude, e.g. the self-weight of a bridge structure and any permanent loads fixed to it

Deck the bridge floor designed to carry the traffic

Distributed Load the uniform or variable load distributed along a bridge

Duct a channel or tube for conveying fluid, cables, etc., especially public utility services

Dynamic or **Live Load** a load that is applied or changes sufficiently rapidly to bring into play significant inertial resistances

Equilibrium the state reached when the forces acting on a body are balanced

Expansion Joint a gap or joint in a structural member (especially concrete) to allow for thermal expansion of the member

Extrados the convex surface of an arch

Fieldstone stone occurring randomly on the surface of the ground in a locality

Fill material, such as gravel, earth or rubble, used to fill the space between spandrels, behind retaining walls, and to construct embankments

Flange a wide flat projection on a structural member, usually at right angles to the main member

Girder a structural component comprising tension and compression flanges connected by bracing or solid web elements

Grouting the filling of the voids in structural elements with a thin fluid mortar or cement

Guniting the application of a layer of mortar or concrete by projecting it at high speed on to a surface

Hanger a vertical tension member connecting the deck of a suspension bridge with the suspended cable

Haunch the part of an arch between the springing and the crown

Hennibique System a system of concrete reinforcement consisting of a combination of alternate straight bars with ends bent up at an angle, with vertical V bars, or stirrups, of flat iron passing around the straight bars and reaching nearly to the top of the beam

Howe Truss a type of lattice girder in which the diagonal bracing elements are in compression

Impost the upper course of a pillar carrying an arch

Intrados the concave surface of an arch

Jack Arch a brick or concrete arch spanning between the flanges of girder for the purpose of transferring loads from the fill to the girders

Kahn System a system of concrete reinforcement in which the square-section have horizontal extensions that are broken away and bent up (or down) to provide bond and resistance to shearing forces

Keystone the voussoir placed last at the crown (top) of an arch

Latticed Girder or **Truss** a metal girder or truss in which the top and bottom flanges are connected by a series of criss-crossing diagonal members

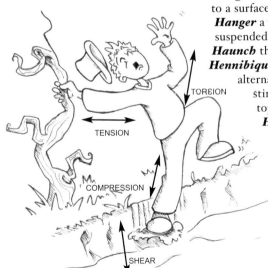

TORSION

TENSION

COMPRESSION

SHEAR

FORCES ACTING ON STRUCTURE

Load the forces applied to a structure

Masonry stonework or the work of a mason

Mass Concrete concrete containing no reinforcement

Mild Steel steel containing a small percentage of carbon, strong and tough, but not easily tempered

Mortar the matrix used in the beds and joints in masonry, to adhere and bind, fill the voids, and distribute the pressures exerted by the loads

Moss Bar reinforcement bar of rail-type section

Oriel decorative circular feature in spandrel wall, normally over a pier

Patrasses metal spreader plates connected by a tie road inserted through the spandrels of a masonry bridge to prevent them from moving outwards

Pediment the triangular part of a building or structure surmounting a series of columns

Pier an intermediate support between two elements of the superstructure of a bridge

Pilaster a rectangular column, especially one projecting from a wall or other vertical surface

Pile a vertical member driven or in some other way placed in the ground to provide vertical support for a structure

Plate Girder a girder in which the top and bottom flanges are connected by a solid vertical web

Portal Frame a frame consisting of two uprights connected at the top by a third member, which may be horizontal, sloping or curved

Post-Tensioning a method of pre-stressing concrete, in which the cables are pulled or the concrete is jacked up after it has been poured

Pratt Truss a girder having a mixture of vertical (compression) and sloping (tension) members connecting the top and bottom flanges

Pre-cast Concrete concrete components that are cast and partly matured on-site or in a factory before being lifted into their position in a structure

Prefabrication the fabrication of structural elements in a factory or on-site yard prior to their being used in a structure

Prestressed Concrete concrete in which cracking and tensile forces are eliminated or greatly reduced by compressing it with stretched cables within it or by pressure from abutments

Pre-tensioning concrete members are pre-cast, usually in a factory, with the tensioned wires embedded in them, the wires are anchored, either against the moulds, or against permanent abutments in the ground. After hardening, the concrete is released from the mould and the wires are cut off at the anchorage

Puddle Clay clay worked to a suitable consistency to form a barrier to the passage of water

Refuge a recess in the parapet wall of a masonry arch bridge, usually built up from a cutwater

Reinforced Concrete concrete containing reinforcement to counter the inherent inability of concrete to resist tensile and shear forces

Reinforcement steel rods or mesh embedded in concrete or plaster or mortar and bonded to it

Relieving Arch an arch designed to remove load from the main structure

Retaining Wall a wall built to prevent the movement of loose material or fill

Rib a band of masonry projecting from the soffit of a masonry arch

Rise the vertical distance from the springings to the crown of an arch

Rolled Steel Joist (RSJ) a solid I-section steel girder passed through a hot-rolling mill

Rubble Stone quarried stones of angular shape and random size

Rusticated Ashlar ashlar on which the face is left rough and stands out from the joints, the stones being cut back at the edges by bevelling or rebating

Segmental Arch one whose intrados is less than a semi-circle

Semi-Circular Arch one whose intrados is a semi-circle

Shear or **Shear Force** a sliding force acting across a beam near its support

Sheet Piles flat timber or trough-section steel piles driven edge to edge to form a vertical barrier against ingress of material or water

Simply Supported in the case of a beam, supported at or near its two ends in such a way that it is free at both of them to rotate in the plane of the loads and free at one of them to expand or contract longitudinally

Skewback the stones forming the slopes on the piers or abutments on which the lowest ring stones rest in segmental arches

Skirt a protective surround to a bridge pier to counter the scouring action of a river

Slab a structural element capable of spanning a horizontal gap in the manner of a beam, but extended laterally

Soffit the underside of an arch or beam

Span the distance between the supports of an arch or beam

Spandrel the space between the extrados of an arch, or two adjacent arches, and the bottom of the road metal or road plates

Springing the lowest point on an arch at which it 'springs' from an abutment or pier

Steel iron in which the carbon content has been reduced by blowing an air blast through the molten metal to increase its strength and improve its ductility

Stiffener a rib-like projection from a thin structural member loaded in compression to increase the stiffness in bending and thereby prevent buckling

Strain the change in shape or dimensions resulting from stress (may be tensile, compressive, or shear)

Stress the effect of load on a structure. Measured as force per unit of resisting area (may be tensile, compressive, or shear)

String Course horizontal courses (sometimes projecting or moulded) built into the faces of walls
to act as a tie or to emphasise the structure

Strut a structural member absorbing a compressive or 'pushing' force

Superstructure the upper part of a bridge, excluding the foundations and at least the lower parts of the piers

Suspender a vertical hanger in a suspension bridge, by which the roadway is carried on the cables

Swing Bridge a bridge that swings open horizontally to allow a ship or barge to pass. It may have one leaf pivoted centrally or two equal leaves pivoted about their ends

Tendon a pre-stressing cable

Tension a pulling force or stress

Three-centred Arch an arch whose intrados comprises portions of three circular arcs

Through-Arch an arch through which the deck passes

Thrust the resultant force in an arch acting towards the abutment

Tie a structural member transmitting a tensile or 'pulling' force

Tie bar a metal rod inserted to counter movement apart of two structural elements

Torsion a twisting force

Truss a framework in which the individual members experience only tension or compression. The truss as a structural component supports loads like a beam or girder

Underpin to excavate beneath the foundation of piers or abutments and extend them downwards in masonry or concrete

Voussoir an arch stone of tapered or wedge shape

Waterway the distance between the end abutments less the sum of the pier thicknesses

Web the material in a girder between the flanges

Wrought-Iron iron made in bars by beating or rolling out the slag and impurities in a semi-molten state on the furnace hearth, thus giving the metal a fibrous structure and improving its ductility or ability to bend

BIBLIOGRAPHY
& PHOTOGRAPHIC CREDITS

Bibliography

Barry, M.B. *Across Deep Waters*. Frankfort Press, Dublin, 1985

Cox, R.C. & Gould, M.H. *Civil Engineering Heritage: Ireland*. London, Thomas Telford Publications, 1998

De Mare, E. *Bridges of Britain*. London, Batsford, 1975

Delany, R. *Ireland's Inland Waterways*. Belfast, Appletree Press, 1992

Johnson, S. *Johnson's Atlas & Gazetteer of the Railways of Ireland*. Leicester, Midland Publishing Ltd.,1997

Maidstone, Roland J (1998) *Developments in Structural Form. 2nd Edition.* Oxford, Architectural Press

McCutcheon, W.A. *The Industrial Archaeology of Northern Ireland*. Belfast, HMSO, 1980

O'Connor, Colin (1985) *Spanning two Centuries. Historic Bridges of Australia.* St. Lucia, Queensland, University of Australia Press

O'Keeffe, P.J. and Simington, T. *Irish Stone Bridges: History and Heritage*. Dublin, Irish Academic Press, 1991

Robb, W. *A History of Northern Ireland Railways*. Belfast, Northern Ireland Railways, 1982

Rowledge, J.W.P. *A Regional History of Railways, Volume 16: Ireland*. Penryn, Atlantic Transport Publishers, 1995

Ruddock, T. *Arch Bridges and their Builders 1735 – 1835*. Cambridge, Cambridge University Press, 1979

Scott, J.S. *A Dictionary of Civil Engineering*. Harmonsworth, Middlesex, Penguin Books, 1958

Walther, R. *Cable-Stayed Bridges*. London, Thomas Telford Publishing, 1999

Photographic Credits

PHOTOGRAPHY IS BY ONE OR OTHER OF THE AUTHORS EXCEPT AS HEREUNDER:

Clonmacnoise Bridge Model: John Scarry/Department of the Environment, Heritage & Local Government

Esler Crawford: Annagola Bridge (Middletown), Cross Harbour Bridges

Office of Public Works: Shannonbridge (Swivel Bridge)

Laganside Development Corporation: Maysfield Lifting Bridge

Institution of Engineers of Ireland: Kilcummer Viaduct, Rathdrum Viaduct

Jim Lyttle: Solitude Park Bridge (Banbridge), Bearney Bridge (Sion Mills), The Point of Whitecoat Bridge (Portadown)

Belfast Harbour Commissioners: Long Bridge (Belfast)

Irish Architectural Archive: Oak Park Bridge (Carlow)

Coleraine Chronicle: Coleraine Lifting Bridge

Iarnród Éireann: Rail over-bridge near Sallins

Arup Consulting Engineers: West Link Toll Bridge

Deane Public Works: Letter Bridge

Commissioners of Irish Lights: Mizen Head Footbridge; Translink: Greenisland Viaduct.

Tara O'Reilly/Meath County Council: New Boyne Bridge

Ronnie Norton (Norton Associates): James Joyce Bridge

Roughan & O'Donovan: Taney Bridge (Dublin), Macken Street Bridge (Dublin)

Department of the Environment, Heritage & Local Government: Brú na Bóinne Footbridge

WDR&RT Taggart: ECOS Footbridge (Ballymena)

GEDA Construction: St Patrick's Footbridge (Omagh)